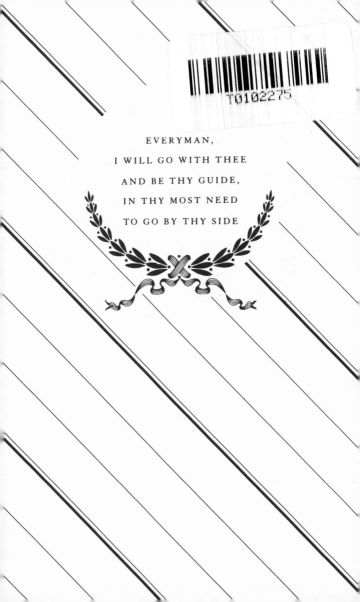

EVERYMAN,
I WILL GO WITH THEE
AND BE THY GUIDE,
IN THY MOST NEED
TO GO BY THY SIDE

EVERYMAN'S LIBRARY
POCKET POETS

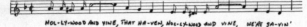

STEPHEN SONDHEIM LYRICS

• • • • • • • • • • • • • • • • • •

EDITED BY
PETER GETHERS

WITH RUSSELL PERREAULT

EVERYMAN'S LIBRARY
POCKET POETS

Alfred A. Knopf   New York   London   Toronto

THIS IS A BORZOI BOOK

PUBLISHED BY ALFRED A. KNOPF

Compilation copyright © 2020 by Stephen Sondheim
Introduction copyright © 2020 by Everyman's Library

All rights reserved. Published in the United States by Alfred A. Knopf, a division of Penguin Random House LLC, New York, and in Canada by Penguin Random House Canada Limited, Toronto. Distributed by Penguin Random House LLC, New York. Published in the United Kingdom by Everyman's Library, 50 Albemarle Street, London W1S 4BD and distributed by Penguin Random House UK, 20 Vauxhall Bridge Road, London SW1V 2SA.

www.randomhouse/everymans
www.everymanslibrary.co.uk

ISBN 978-1-101-90816-7 (US)
978-1-84159-818-5 (UK)

A CIP catalogue record for this book is available from the British Library

Typography by Peter B. Willberg

Typeset in the UK by Input Data Services, Isle Abbotts, Somerset

Printed and bound in Germany
by GGP Media GmbH, Possneck

CONTENTS

INTRODUCTION

Nearly fifteen years ago, I was lucky enough to be at a dinner with Stephen Sondheim. I was not – and am not – a huge fan of musical theater but was – and am even more so now – what can only be described as a "Sondheim fanatic." I saw the original Broadway production of *Company* when I was a teenager and it completely altered my view of not only what musicals could do but of what theater was capable of doing. The show was angry, dark, cynical, funny and reflected the angst of that period as well as the anguish, humor and thrill of relationships in a profound and stunning way. It was life-changing.

For some inexplicable reason, I missed seeing *Follies* and *Merrily We Roll Along* in their initial runs, but have seen every other original Broadway production of Stephen's shows. I saw the first version of his collaboration with James Lapine, *Sunday in the Park with George*, twice and that's when my fanaticism kicked into an even higher gear. It was unquestionably the greatest night of theater I had ever experienced and having now attended various productions over the years, that opinion holds. I've not only traveled to cities around this country to see local productions of Sondheim shows (the Philadelphia version of *Assassins* was particularly memorable, with the assassination of Lincoln taking place in the actual balcony of the theater), I went to London several times so I wouldn't miss specific productions and performances (such as Judi Dench in *A Little Night Music* and Imelda Staunton in *Gypsy*).

At that initial dinner were two longtime Sondheim friends – William Goldman, who had known him pre-*West Side Story*, and Frank Rich, who had arranged the evening – and various spouses and companions. I learned that Sondheim shared my taste for noir movies and for Alan Ayckbourn's plays, and got to hear stories about six-room apartments on Manhattan's Upper West Side in the 1950s for $200 a month, and script-doctoring Broadway shows during out-of-town try-outs, and something I never knew existed: anonymous song-doctoring for Broadway musicals, which Sondheim had done in his youth to pick up some spare change and get a taste of the glamorous theater life. As a dutiful book editor, I asked the great man why he had never collected all his lyrics in a single volume. His answer was a tad surprising: "My ultimate nightmare is to see all my lyrics in one place."

Undeterred by this seeming roadblock, I began to send pestering notes every three months or so, reintroducing myself, reminding him of our dinner together, and asking if he was ready to do a book of his lyrics. In response, I would get a handwritten note that basically and always politely thanked me and ended with a firm no. Then, nearly three years later, my assistant appeared in my doorway and said, breathlessly, "Stephen Sondheim just called and asked for your email address." I calmly said, "Well, give it to him." Several minutes later, a chapter arrived in my email inbox. Fittingly, the pages were about *Company*, and it was not just a collection of lyrics, it was a very personal history of the production and analysis of many of the songs and even a bit of autobiography. That chapter was chosen to try first because the author thought it would be the hardest for him to write and would prove that his prose was not worthy of a full-fledged book. The author was, of course, as wrong as he could possibly be, and that chapter eventually became, over the course of a few years, two full volumes, *Finishing the Hat* and *Look, I Made a Hat* and I believe, along with Moss Hart's *Act One* and Goldman's *The Season*, they are the best and most valuable books ever written and published about the theater.

Working with Stephen was a pleasure and an education. The process was largely my asking questions that he usually answered, my making comments that he usually told me were wrong, and my arguing that he was too hard on his own lyrics and that his self-criticisms weren't correct, arguments I won on a few occasions.

While working together, here are a few of the things I learned about his lyric-writing and his writing process:

– His overriding mantra is that God is in the details, and he will ponder and analyze those details until he gets as close to perfection as possible. Perhaps the best example of this is in the song "Losing My Mind." Look at the difference in impact the shift from "and" to "to" has in the following stanza:

> I dim the lights
> And think about you,
> Spend sleepless nights
> To think about you.
> You said you loved me,
> Or were you just being kind?
> Or am I losing my mind?

It would have been easy to repeat the word "and" but the shift creates such a higher level of anxiety and passion and obsession. The detail completely changes the level of turbulence in the song.

– Mr. Sondheim doesn't like cleverness for the sake of being clever. His lyrical cleverness must be character-driven ("A Little Priest") or must come from the fact that he is trying to write within a particular song style or genre ("The Story of Lucy and Jessie").

– He believes – no, insists – that lyrics are not poetry. One reason impossible to argue with is that lyrics are not written in a vacuum; they are written to go with music. True. But here is the OED definition of poetry:

"noun. A piece of writing in which the expression of feelings and ideas is given intensity by particular attention to diction (sometimes involving rhyme), rhythm, and imagery." So I don't get another email from Mr. Sondheim with the words "You are wrong" in the heading, I will let the readers decide for themselves if the words in this collection qualify as poetry. Read them in this collection or read them in their entirety in the two more complete books or listen to them with their accompanying music (mostly also Mr. Sondheim's). I'm fairly sure I know on which side of the fence you will alight.

– For someone who I believe is the most emotionally devastating lyricist who ever lived (if you don't like the sound of hysterical sobbing, try not to be anywhere in the vicinity if I am listening to "Children and Art"), he maintains a curious emotional distance from his own lyrics, vehemently maintaining that he writes only from the character's perspective, not from his own. Do I believe this? Not really. At least not entirely. Yes, the emotional range of his lyrics is astonishing and worthy of an enormous crowd with disparate views. And while the melancholy of "Beautiful" may belong to Seurat's mother, and the plaintiveness of "Children Will Listen" may belong to the Witch, and the bitterness of "Could I Leave You?" certainly belongs to Phyllis, and the loneliness of "I Wish I Could Forget You" emanates from both Giorgio and Fosca, and the genuine frivolity of "Comedy Tonight" bubbles out of Pseudolus, and the magnificent combination of cynicism and celebration of "Being Alive" comes from the soul of Bobby, they all can only belong to the genius, demons, love, and yes, poetry that all live inside Stephen Sondheim.

PETER GETHERS

SATURDAY NIGHT

Love's a Bond

VOCALIST

I'm smart as a fox
With bonds and with stocks;
I've cornered wheat, alfalfa and rye.
But now I'm tired of
That hue and cry.
Consolidated Love
Is all I buy.

When put to the test,
I like to invest,
But I won't be a great financier.
Love's the stock I like,
It's free and clear,
And it'll be blue chip
If you chip
In with me, my dear.

Love's a bond that's pure.
Its dividends are sure.
This bond, if you get it,
Is stable and yet it
Will grow if you let it
Mature.

And darling, have you heard?
The market's spiraling like a bird!
As A.T.&T. will,
Go up and up, we will,
For this new love of ours
Is gilt-edged preferred.

WEST SIDE STORY

Gee, Officer Krupke

ACTION

Dear kindly Sergeant Krupke,
You gotta understand:
It's just our bringin' upke
That gets us outta hand.
Our mothers all are junkies,
Our fathers all are drunks.

ALL

Golly Moses, natcherly we're punks!

Gee, Officer Krupke, we're very upset:
We never had the love that every
    child oughta get.
We ain't no delinquents,
We're misunderstood.
Deep down inside us there is good!

ACTION

There is good!

ALL

There is good, there is good,
There is untapped good.
Like inside, the worst of us is good.

SNOWBOY

That's a touchin' good story.

ACTION

Lemme tell it to the world!

SNOWBOY

Just tell it to the judge.

ACTION

Dear kindly Judge, your Honor,
My parents treat me rough.
With all their marijuana,
They won't give me a puff.
They didn't wanna have me,
But somehow I was had.
Leapin' lizards, that's why I'm so bad!

DIESEL

Right!
Officer Krupke, you're really a square.
This boy don't need a judge, he needs a [*sic*]
 analyst's care.
It's just his neurosis that oughta be curbed.
He's psychologically disturbed!

ACTION

I'm disturbed!

ALL

We're disturbed, we're disturbed,

We're the most disturbed.
Like we're psychologically disturbed.

> DIESEL
>
> In the opinion of this court, this child is depraved
> on account he ain't had a normal home.

> ACTION
>
> Hey, I'm depraved on account I'm deprived!

> DIESEL
>
> So take him to a head shrinker.

> ACTION

My father is a bastard,
My ma's an S.O.B.
My grandpa's always plastered,
My grandma pushes tea.

My sister wears a mustache,
My brother wears a dress.
Goodness gracious, that's why I'm a mess!

> A-RAB

Yes!
Officer Krupke, you're really a slob.
This boy don't need a doctor, just a good
     honest job.
Society's played him a terrible trick,
And sociologically he's sick!

ACTION

I am sick!

ALL

We are sick, we are sick,
We are sick, sick, sick,
Like we're sociologically sick!

A-RAB

In my opinion, this child don't need to have his head shrunk at all. Juvenile delinquency is purely a social disease.

ACTION

Hey, I got a social disease!

A-RAB

So take him to a social worker!

ACTION

Dear kindly social worker,
They say go earn a buck,
Like be a soda jerker,
Which means like be a schmuck.
It's not I'm anti-social,
I'm only anti-work.
Gloryosky, that's why I'm a jerk!

BABY JOHN

Eek!
Officer Krupke, you've done it again.

This boy don't need a job, he needs a year in
the pen.
It ain't just a question of misunderstood—
Deep down inside him he's no good!

ACTION
I'm no good!

ALL
We're no good, we're no good,
We're no earthly good,
Like the best of us is no damn good!

DIESEL
The trouble is he's crazy.

A-RAB
The trouble is he drinks.

BABY JOHN
The trouble is he's lazy.

DIESEL
The trouble is he stinks.

A-RAB
The trouble is he's growing.

BABY JOHN
The trouble is he's grown!

Krupke, we got troubles of our own!

Gee, Officer Krupke,
We're down on our knees,
'Cause no one wants a fella with a social disease.
Gee, Officer Krupke,
What are we to do?
Gee, Officer Krupke—
Krup you!

Cool

Boy, boy, crazy boy,
Get cool, boy.
Gotta rocket
In your pocket,
Keep coolly cool, boy.

Don't get hot,
'Cause, man, you got
Some high times ahead.
Take it slow,
And Daddy-o,
You can live it up and die in bed.

Boy, boy, crazy boy,
Stay loose, boy.
Breeze it, buzz it,
Easy does it,
Turn off the juice, boy.

Go, man, go,
But not like a yoyo schoolboy.
Just play it cool, boy,
Real cool.

Somewhere

There's a place for us,
Somewhere a place for us.
Peace and quiet and open air
Wait for us, somewhere.

There's a time for us,
Some day a time for us,
Time together with time to spare,
Time to learn, time to care.

Some day,
Somewhere,
We'll find a new way of living,
We'll find a way of forgiving.
Somewhere,
Somewhere . . .

There's a place for us,
A time and place for us.
Hold my hand and we're halfway there.
Hold my hand and I'll take you there
Some day,
Somehow,
Somewhere!

GYPSY

Momma's Talkin' Soft
(*cut from the show*)

BABY JUNE, LOUISE
Momma's talkin' soft,
Momma's got a plan.
Momma's eyes are wide,
Momma's seen a man.

Momma's blushin' pink,
Fluffin' up her hair.
Momma has a smile—
And when she has a smile,
No one else has a prayer.

Momma's talkin' low,
Momma's gonna win.
Momma's movin' slow,
Momma's movin' in.

Bet when Momma's done,
Not a soul survives.
Momma's talkin' soft,
Everybody run for your lives.

Rose's Turn

ROSE

With what I have in me, I could've been better than ANY OF YOU! What I got in me – what I been holding down inside of me – if I ever let it out, there wouldn't be signs big enough! There wouldn't be lights bright enough!

(*The orchestra plays a chord*)

Here she is, boys!

(*And another*)

Here she is, world!

(*And another*)

Here's Rose!!

Curtain up!
Light the lights!

Play it, boys!

You either got it,
Or you ain't,—
And, boys, I got it!
You like it?

ORCHESTRA

Yeah!

ROSE

Well, I got it!

Some people got it and make it pay,
Some people can't even give it away!
This people's got it,
And this people's spreadin' it around.
You either have it—
Or you've had it.

Hello, everybody! My name's Rose.
What's yours?

(Strutting like a stripper)

How d'ya like them egg rolls, Mr. Goldstone?

Hold your hats and Hallelujah,
Momma's gonna show it to ya!
Momma's talkin' loud,
Momma's doin' fine!
Momma's gettin' hot,
Momma's goin' strong,
Momma's movin' on!
Momma's all alone,
Momma doesn't care,
Momma's lettin' loose,

Momma's got the stuff,
Momma's lettin' go—

(*Stammering*)

M-M-Momma—

(*Again*)

M-M-Momma—

(*Recovering*)

Momma's got the stuff,
Momma's gotta move,
Momma's gotta go—
M-Momma—
M-Momma's—
Momma's gotta let go!

Why did I do it? What did it get me?
Scrapbooks full of me in the background.
Give 'em love and what does it get you?
What does it get you?
One quick look as each of 'em leaves you!
All your life and what does it get you?
Thanks a lot, and out with the garbage!
They take bows and you're battin' zero!

I had a dream—
I dreamed it for you, June.
It wasn't for me, Herbie.
And if it wasn't for me,
Then where would you be,
Miss Gypsy Rose Lee?!

Well, someone tell me, when is it my turn?
Don't I get a dream for myself?
Startin' now, it's gonna be my turn!
Gangway, world, get off of my runway!
Startin' now, I bat a thousand!
This time, boys, I'm takin' the bows and
Everything's coming up Rose!
Everything's coming up roses!
Everything's coming up roses
This time for me!
For me!
For me!
For me!
For me!
FOR ME!!

A FUNNY THING HAPPENED ON THE WAY TO THE FORUM

Comedy Tonight

PROLOGUS
Something familiar,
Something peculiar,
Something for everyone – a comedy tonight!
Something appealing,
Something appalling,
Something for everyone – a comedy tonight!

Nothing with kings,
Nothing with crowns,
Bring on the lovers, liars and clowns.

Old situations,
New complications,
Nothing portentous or polite.
Tragedy tomorrow,
Comedy tonight!

(*The Proteans [three male performers who play
numerous parts during the show] enter*)

PROLOGUS
Something convulsive,
Something repulsive,
Something for everyone – a comedy tonight!

Something esthetic,

PROTEANS
Something frenetic,

PROLOGUS
Something for everyone – a comedy tonight!

PROTEANS
Nothing with gods,
Nothing with fate.

PROLOGUS
Weighty affairs will just have to wait.

PROTEANS
Nothing that's formal,

PROLOGUS
Nothing that's normal,

ALL
No recitations to recite!
Open up the curtain—
Comedy tonight!

Something erratic,
Something dramatic,
Something for everyone – a comedy tonight!

Frenzy and frolic,
Strictly symbolic,
Something for everyone – a comedy tonight!

(*The entire Company enters*)

ALL
Something familiar,
Something peculiar,
Something for everybody – comedy tonight!

Something that's gaudy,
Something that's bawdy,
Something for everybawdy – comedy tonight!

Nothing that's grim,
Nothing that's Greek,

PROLOGUS
(*Referring to a tall, buxom young woman*)
She plays Medea later this week.

ALL
Stunning surprises,
Cunning disguises,
Hundreds of actors out of sight!

(Variously)

Pantaloons and tunics,
Courtesans and eunuchs,
Funerals and chases,
Baritones and basses,
Panderers,
Philanderers,
Cupidity,
Timidity,
Mistakes,
Fakes,
Rhymes,
Mimes,
Tumblers,
Grumblers,
Fumblers,
Bumblers,

ALL
No royal curse,
No Trojan horse,
And a happy ending, of course!

Goodness and badness,
Man in his madness,
This time it all turns out all right—
Tragedy tomorrow,
Comedy tonight!

ANYONE CAN WHISTLE

Anyone Can Whistle

FAY

Anyone can whistle,
That's what they say—
Easy.
Anyone can whistle,
Any old day—
Easy.

It's all so simple:
Relax, let go, let fly.
So someone tell me why
Can't I?

I can dance a tango,
I can read Greek—
Easy.
I can slay a dragon
Any old week—
Easy.

What's hard is simple,
What's natural comes hard.
Maybe you could show me
How to let go,

Lower my guard,
Learn to be free.
Maybe if you whistle,
Whistle for me.

A Hero Is Coming
(*cut from the play*)

FAY
(*To Schub and Cooley*)
A hero is coming.
You won't know him by his white
Charger,
But he'll be the kind of knight
That we need.
A hero is coming.
No, you won't hear any band
Playing,
But he's gonna take a stand
And succeed!

(*To the Cookies*)

Never fear,
He'll be here in time.
Heroes don't appear
Till the nick of time.

(*Referring to Schub and Cooley*)

Who are they?
Let them plot and plan.
Let them have their day

And their way
While they can,

(*To Schub and Cooley*)

'Cause a hero is coming,
Coming quietly with no
Trumpets,
But he'll be here any mo-
Ment, so fly, boys,
Fly!
You won't know him by his bright
Armor,
But there'll be a funny light
In his eye, boys!

Stars won't burst,
Mountains will not crash,
Thunder won't come first
And no lightning will flash.
Oh, maybe an aura—
One tiny glow—
Maybe the faintest drums.

But a hero is coming,
That much I know,
And we're not gonna do a thing till he comes!

Everybody Says Don't

HAPGOOD

Everybody says don't,
Everybody says don't,
Everybody says don't, it isn't right,
Don't, it isn't nice!

Everybody says don't,
Everybody says don't,
Everybody says don't walk on the grass,
Don't disturb the peace,
Don't skate on the ice.

Well, I say
Do!
I say
Walk on the grass, it was meant to feel!
I say
Sail!
Tilt at the windmill,
And if you fail, you fail.

Everybody says don't,
Everybody says don't,
Everybody says don't get out of line.
When they say that, then,
Lady, that's a sign:
Nine times out of ten,
Lady, you are doing just fine!

Make just a ripple.
Come on, be brave.
This time a ripple,
Next time a wave.
Sometimes you have to start small,
Climbing the tiniest wall,
Maybe you're going to fall,
But it's better than not starting at all!

Everybody says no,
Everybody says stop,
Everybody says mustn't rock the boat,
Mustn't touch a thing.

Everybody says don't,
Everybody says wait,
Everybody says can't fight City Hall,
Can't upset the cart,
Can't laugh at the King!

Well, I say,
Try!
I say,
Laugh at the kings or they'll make you cry.

Lose your
Poise.
Fall if you have to,
But, lady, make a noise!

Everybody says don't.
Everybody says can't.
Everybody says wait around for miracles,
That's the way the world is made.

I insist on miracles, if *you* do them!
Miracles – nothing to them!
I say don't—
Don't be afraid!

DO I HEAR A WALTZ?

Do I Hear a Waltz?

LEONA
Do I hear a waltz?
Very odd, but I hear a waltz.
There isn't a band
And I don't understand
It at all.

I can't hear a waltz—
Oh, my Lord, there it goes again!
Why is nobody dancing in the street?
Can't they hear the beat?

Magical, mystical miracle,
Can it be? Is it true?
Things are impossibly lyrical.
Is it me? No, it's you!

I do hear a waltz!
I see you and I hear a waltz!
It's what I've been waiting for
All my life, to hear a waltz!

Do you hear a waltz?
Oh, my dear, don't you hear a waltz?
Such lovely Blue Danubey

Music, how can you be
Still?

You *must* hear a waltz!
Even strangers are dancing now:
An old lady is waltzing in her flat,
Waltzing with her cat.

Roses are dancing with peonies.
Yes, it's true! Don't you see?
Everything's suddenly Viennese,
Can't be you! Must be me!

Do I hear a waltz?
I want more than to hear a waltz:
I want you to share it 'cause
Oh, boy, *do* I hear a waltz!
I hear a waltz!
I hear a waltz!

Someone Like You

DI ROSSI

We waited for someone,
But somehow we never
Had looked for someone like you.
Our chances were many,
But we were too clever,
We wanted someone like you.

Suddenly, the door,
Wonderful surprise!
Wonderful and more,
Before
Our eyes.

We thought that surprises
Were over forever,
And then came someone like you.

Take the Moment

DI ROSSI

Take the moment,
Let it happen.
Hug the moment,
Make it last.

Hold the feeling
For the moment,
Or the moment
Will have passed.

All the noises buzzing in your head,
Warning you to wait—
What for?
Don't listen!

Let it happen,
Take the moment.
Make the moment
Many moments more.

Make for us a thousand more.

EVENING PRIMROSE

I Remember

ELLA

I remember sky,
It was blue as ink.
Or at least I think
I remember sky.

I remember snow,
Soft as feathers,
Sharp as thumbtacks,
Coming down like lint,
And it made you squint
When the wind would blow.

And ice, like vinyl, on the streets,
Cold as silver, white as sheets.
Rain, like strings,
And changing things,
Like leaves.

I remember leaves,
Green as spearmint,
Crisp as paper.
I remember trees,
Bare as coat racks,
Spread like broken umbrellas . . .

And parks and bridges,
Ponds and zoos,
Ruddy faces,
Muddy shoes,
Light and noise
And bees and boys
And days.

I remember days,
Or at least I try.
But as years go by,
They're a sort of haze.
And the bluest ink
Isn't really sky,
And at times I think
I would gladly die
For a day of sky.

COMPANY

The Little Things You Do Together

JOANNE

It's the little things you do together,
Do together,
Do together,
That make perfect relationships.
The hobbies you pursue together,
Savings you accrue together,
Looks you misconstrue together
That make marriage a joy.
Mm-hm . . .

It's the little things you share together,
Swear together,
Wear together,
That make perfect relationships,
The concerts you enjoy together,
Neighbors you annoy together,
Children you destroy together,
That keep marriage intact.

It's not so hard to be married
When two maneuver as one.
It's not so hard to be married,
And, Jesus Christ, is it fun.

It's sharing little winks together,
Drinks together,
Kinks together,
That makes marriage a joy.
It's bargains that you shop together,
Cigarettes you stop together,
Clothing that you swap together
That make perfect relationships.
Uh-huh . . .
Mm-hm . . .

ALL
It's not talk of God and the decade ahead that
Allows you to get through the worst.
It's "I do" and "You don't" and "Nobody said
      that"
And "Who brought the subject up first?"

It's the little things,
The little little little little little things . . .

JENNY, DAVID, AMY, PAUL
The little ways you try together—

SUSAN, PETER, JOANNE, LARRY
Cry together—

JENNY, DAVID, AMY, PAUL
Lie together—

GROUP
That make perfect relationships.

SUSAN, PETER, JOANNE, LARRY
Becoming a cliché together—

JENNY, DAVID, AMY, PAUL
Growing old and gray together—

JOANNE
Withering away together—

GROUP
That makes marriage a joy.

MEN, JOANNE
It's not so hard to be married.

WOMEN
It's much the cleanest of crimes.

MEN, JOANNE
It's not so hard to be married,

JOANNE
I've done it three or four times.

JENNY
It's people that you hate together,

PAUL, AMY
Bait together,

PETER, SUSAN
Date together,

GROUP
That make marriage a joy.

DAVID
It's things like using force together,

LARRY
Shouting till you're hoarse together,

JOANNE
Getting a divorce together,

GROUP
That make perfect relationships.
Uh-huh . . .
Kiss, kiss . . .

JOANNE
Mm-hm.

The Ladies Who Lunch

JOANNE

Here's to the ladies who lunch—
Everybody laugh—
Lounging in their caftans and planning a brunch
On their own behalf.

Off to the gym,
Then to a fitting,
Claiming they're fat,
And looking grim
'Cause they've been sitting
Choosing a hat.

Does anyone still wear a hat?

I'll drink to that.

Here's to the girls who stay smart—
Aren't they a gas?
Rushing to their classes in optical art,
Wishing it would pass.

Another long exhausting day,
Another thousand dollars,
A matinee, a Pinter play,
Perhaps a piece of Mahler's—
I'll drink to that.

And one for Mahler.

Here's to the girls who play wife—
Aren't they too much?
Keeping house, but clutching a copy of *Life*
Just to keep in touch.

The ones who follow the rules
And meet themselves at the schools,
Too busy to know that they're fools—
Aren't they a gem?
I'll drink to them.
Let's all drink to them!

And here's to the girls who just watch—
Aren't they the best?
When they get depressed, it's a bottle of Scotch,
Plus a little jest.

Another chance to disapprove,
Another brilliant zinger,
Another reason not to move,
Another vodka stinger—
Aaaaahhhhhh—

I'll drink to that.

So here's to the girls on the go—
Everybody tries.
Look into their eyes
And you'll see what they know:
Everybody dies.

A toast to that invincible bunch,
The dinosaurs surviving the crunch—
Let's hear it for the ladies who lunch!
Everybody rise! Rise!
Rise! Rise! Rise! Rise! Rise! Rise! Rise!

Being Alive

ROBERT

Someone to hold you too close,
Someone to hurt you too deep,
Someone to sit in your chair,
To ruin your sleep . . .

Someone to need you too much,
Someone to know you too well,
Someone to pull you up short
To put you through hell . . .

Someone you have to let in,
Someone whose feelings you spare,
Someone who, like it or not,
Will want you to share
A little a lot . . .

Someone to crowd you with love,
Someone to force you to care,
Someone to make you come through,
Who'll always be there,
As frightened as you
Of being alive,
Being alive, being alive, being alive.

Somebody hold me too close,
Somebody hurt me too deep,
Somebody sit in my chair

And ruin my sleep
And make me aware
Of being alive, being alive.

Somebody need me too much,
Somebody know me too well,
Somebody pull me up short
And put me through hell
And give me support
For being alive.
Make me alive,
Make me alive.

Make me confused,
Mock me with praise,
Let me be used,
Vary my days.
But alone is alone, not alive.

Somebody crowd me with love,
Somebody force me to care,
Somebody let me come through,
I'll always be there
As frightened as you,
To help us survive
Being alive, being alive,
Being alive!

Multitudes of Amys
(*cut from show*)

ROBERT
Multitudes of Amys
Crowd the streets below;
Avenues of Amys,
Officefuls of Amys,
Everywhere I go.
Wonder what it means—
Ho-ho, I wonder what it means:
I see them waiting for the lights,
Running for the bus,
Milling in the stores,
And hailing cabs
And disappearing through revolving doors.

Multitudes of Amys
Everywhere I look,
Sentences of Amys,
Paragraphs of Amys
Filling every book.
Wonder if it means I've gone to pieces.
Every other word I speak is something she says.
Walls hang with pictures of Amys,
Galaxies of Amys dot the night skies.
Girls pass and look at me with Amy's eyes.
I've seen an audience of Amys
Watch a cast of Amys act in a play.

Seems there are more of her every day.
What can it mean?
What can it mean?

I've caught a stadium of Amys
Standing up to cheer,
Choruses of Amys,
Symphonies of Amys
Ringing in my ear.
I know what it means—
Hey, Amy, I know what it means!
Oh, wow!
I'm ready, I'm ready, I'm ready
Now!

All that it takes is two, Amy,
Me, Amy,
You, Amy . . .
I know what it means—
Hey, Amy, I know what it means!
I'm ready, I'm ready, I'll say it:
Marry me now!

Marry Me a Little

ROBERT

Marry me a little,
Love me just enough.
Cry, but not too often,
Play, but not too rough.
Keep a tender distance,
So we'll both be free.
That's the way it ought to be.
I'm ready!

Marry me a little,
Do it with a will.
Make a few demands
I'm able to fulfill.
Want me more than others,
Not exclusively.
That's the way it ought to be.
I'm ready!
I'm ready now!

You can be my best friend,
I can be your right arm.
We'll go through a fight or two.
No harm, no harm.
We'll look not too deep,
We'll go not too far.
We won't have to give up a thing,

We'll stay who we are.
Right?
Okay, then,
I'm ready!
I'm ready now!

Amy,
Marry me a little,
Love me just enough.
Warm and sweet and easy,
Just the simple stuff.
Keep a tender distance
So we'll both be free.
That's the way it ought to be.
I'm ready!

Marry me a little,
Body, heart and soul.
Passionate as hell,
But always in control.
Want me first and foremost,
Keep me company.
That's the way it ought to be.
I'm ready!
I'm ready now!

Oh, how gently we'll talk,
Oh, how softly we'll tread.
All the stings, the ugly things

We'll keep unsaid.
We'll build a cocoon
Of love and respect.
You promise whatever you like,
I'll never collect.
Right?
Okay, then,
I'm ready!
I'm ready now!
Someone,
I'm ready!

FOLLIES

The Road You Didn't Take

BEN

You're either a poet
Or you're a lover,
Or you're the famous
Benjamin Stone.

You take one road,
You try one door,
There isn't time for any more.
One's life consists of either/or.
One has regrets,
Which one forgets,
And as the years go on,
The road you didn't take
Hardly comes to mind,
Does it?
The door you didn't try,
Where could it have led?

The choice you didn't make
Never was defined,
Was it?
Dreams you didn't dare
Are dead.
Were they ever there?

Who said?
I don't remember,
I don't remember
At all . . .

The books I'll never read
Wouldn't change a thing,
Would they?
The girls I'll never know
I'm too tired for.

The lives I'll never lead
Couldn't make me sing,
Could they?
Could they?
Could they?

Chances that you miss,
Ignore.
Ignorance is bliss—
What's more,
You won't remember,
You won't remember
At all,
Not at all . . .

You yearn for the women,
Long for the money,
Envy the famous
Benjamin Stones.

You take your road,
The decades fly,
The yearnings fade, the longings die.
You learn to bid them all goodbye.
And oh, the peace,
The blessed peace . . .
At last you come to know:

The roads you never take
Go through rocky ground,
Don't they?
The choices that you make
Aren't all that grim.

The worlds you never see
Still will be around,
Won't they?
The Ben I'll never be,
Who remembers him?

Who's That Woman?

STELLA

Who's that woman? I know her well,
All decked out head to toe.
She lives life like a carousel,
Beau after beau after beau.
Nightly, daily,
Always laughing gaily,
Seems I see her everywhere I go.
Oh—

Who's that woman?
I know I know that woman,
So clever
But ever
So sad.
Love, she said, was a fad.
The kind of love that she couldn't make fun of,
She'd have none of.

Who's that woman,
That cheery, weary woman
Who's dressing for yet one more spree?
Each day I see her pass
In my looking glass—
Lord, Lord, Lord, that woman is me!

Mirror, mirror, on the wall,
Who's the saddest gal in town?
Who's been riding for a fall?
Whose Lothario let her down?
Mirror, mirror, answer me:
Who is she who plays the clown?

Is she out each night till three?
Does she laugh with too much glee?
On reflection, she'd agree.
Mirror, mirror,
Mirror, mirror,
Mirror, mirror . . .

STELLA
Who's that woman?
I mean
I've seen

That woman, who's joking
But choking
Back tears.
All those glittering years,
She thought that
Love was a matter of
"Hi, there!" "Kiss me!"

DANCERS
Mirror, mirror,
  on the wall,
Who's the saddest
  gal in town?

Who's been
Riding for a fall?
Love was a matter of
"Hi, there!"
"Kiss me!"

"Bye, there!"   "Bye, there!"

Who's that woman,   Mirror, mirror,
That cheery, weary   Answer me.
  woman
Who's dressing for yet one   Who is she who plays
More spree?   the clown?
The vision's getting
  blurred.
Isn't that absurd?
Lord, Lord, Lord!   Lord, Lord, Lord!
Lord, Lord, Lord,   Mirror, mirror!
  Lord, Lord!
That woman is me.   Mirror, mirror!
That woman is me,   Mirror, mirror!
That woman is me!   Mirror!

66

I'm Still Here

CARLOTTA

Good times and bum times,
I've seen them all and, my dear,
I'm still here.
Plush velvet sometimes,
Sometimes just pretzels and beer,
But I'm here.

I've stuffed the dailies
In my shoes,
Strummed ukuleles,
Sung the blues,
Seen all my dreams disappear,
But I'm here.

I've slept in shanties,
Guest of the W.P.A.,
But I'm here.
Danced in my scanties,
Three bucks a night was the pay,
But I'm here.
I've stood on bread lines
With the best,
Watched while the headlines
Did the rest.
In the depression was I depressed?
Nowhere near.

I met a big financier
And I'm here.

I've been through Gandhi,
Windsor and Wally's affair,
And I'm here.
Amos 'n' Andy,
Mahjongg and platinum hair,
And I'm here.

I got through *Abie's*
Irish Rose,
Five Dionne babies,
Major Bowes,
Had heebie-jeebies
For Beebe's
Bathysphere.
I've lived through Brenda Frazier,
And I'm here.

I've gotten through Herbert and J. Edgar
    Hoover,
Gee, that was fun and a half.
When you've been through Herbert and J. Edgar
    Hoover,
Anything else is a laugh.

I've been through Reno,
I've been through Beverly Hills,
And I'm here.

Reefers and vino,
Rest cures, religion and pills,
And I'm here.

Been called a pinko
Commie tool,
Got through it stinko
By my pool.
I should have gone to an acting school,
That seems clear.
Still, someone said, "She's sincere,"
So I'm here.

Black sable one day,
Next day it goes into hock,
But I'm here.
Top billing Monday,
Tuesday you're touring in stock,
But I'm here.

First you're another
Sloe-eyed vamp,
Then someone's mother,
Then you're camp.
Then you career
From career to career.
I'm almost through my memoirs,
And I'm here.

I've gotten through "Hey, lady, aren't you
    whoozis?
Wow, what a looker you were."
Or, better yet, "Sorry, I thought you were
    whoozis—
What ever happened to her?"

Good times and bum times,
I've seen them all and, my dear,
I'm still here.
Plush velvet sometimes,
Sometimes just pretzels and beer,
But I'm here.
I've run the gamut,
A to Z.
Three cheers and dammit,
C'est la vie.
I got through all of last year,
And I'm here.
Lord knows, at least I've been there,
And I'm here!
Look who's here!
I'm still here!

Could I Leave You?

PHYLLIS
Leave you? Leave you?
How could I leave you?
How could I go it alone?
Could I wave the years away
With a quick goodbye?
How do you wipe tears away
When your eyes are dry?

Sweetheart, lover,
Could I recover,
Give up the joys I have known?
Not to fetch your pills again
Every day at five,
Not to give those dinners for ten
Elderly men
From the U.N.—
How could I survive?

Could I leave you
And your shelves of the World's Best Books,
And the evenings of martyred looks,
Cryptic sighs,
Sullen glares from those injured eyes?
Leave the quips with a sting, jokes with a sneer,
Passionless love-making once a year?
Leave the lies ill-concealed

And the wounds never healed
And the games not worth winning
And – wait, I'm just beginning!

What, leave you, leave you,
How could I leave you?
What would I do on my own?
Putting thoughts of you aside
In the South of France,
Would I think of suicide?
Darling, shall we dance?

Could I live through the pain
On a terrace in Spain?
Would it pass?
It would pass.
Could I bury my rage
With a boy half your age
In the grass?
Bet your ass.
But I've done that already—
Or didn't you know, love?
Tell me, how could I leave
When I left long ago, love?

Could I leave you?
No, the point is, could you leave me?
Well, I guess you could leave me the house,

Leave me the flat,
Leave me the Braques and Chagalls and all that.

You could leave me the stocks for sentiment's
    sake
And ninety percent of the money you make,
And the rugs
And the cooks—
Darling, you keep the drugs,
Angel, you keep the books.
Honey, I'll take the grand,
Sugar, you keep the spinet
And all of our friends and—

Just wait a goddamned minute!

Oh,
Leave you? Leave you?
How could I leave you?
Sweetheart, I have to confess:
Could I leave you?
Yes.
Will I leave you?
Will *I* leave *you*?
Guess!

Losing My Mind

SALLY

The sun comes up,
I think about you.
The coffee cup,
I think about you.
I want you so,
It's like I'm losing my mind.

The morning ends,
I think about you.
I talk to friends,
I think about you.
And do they know
It's like I'm losing my mind?

All afternoon,
Doing every little chore,
The thought of you stays bright.
Sometimes I stand in the middle of the floor,
Not going left,
Not going right.

I dim the lights
And think about you,
Spend sleepless nights
To think about you.
You said you loved me,
Or were you just being kind?
Or am I losing my mind?

The Story of Lucy and Jessie

PHYLLIS

Here's a little story that should make you cry,
About two unhappy dames.
Let us call them Lucy "X" and Jessie "Y,"
Which are not their real names.

Now Lucy has the purity
Along with the unsurety
That comes from being only twenty-one.
Jessie has maturity
And plenty of security,
Whatever you can do with them she's done.

Given their advantages,
You may ask why
The two ladies have such grief.
This is my belief,
In brief:

Lucy is juicy,
But terribly drab.
Jessie is dressy,
But cold as a slab.
Lucy wants to be dressy,
Jessie wants to be juicy.
Lucy wants to be Jessie,
And Jessie, Lucy.
You see,

Jessie is racy,
But hard as a rock.
Lucy is lacy,
But dull as a smock.
Jessie wants to be lacy,
Lucy wants to be Jessie.
That's the sorrowful précis,
It's very messy.

Poor, sad souls,
Itching to be switching roles.
Lucy wants to do what Jessie does,
Jessie wants to be what Lucy was.

Lucy's a lassie
You pat on the head.
Jessie is classy,
But virtually dead.
Lucy wants to be classy,
Jessie wants to be Lassie.
If Lucy and Jessie could only combine,
I could tell you someone
Who would finally feel just fine.

CHORUS
Now if you see Lucy "X,"
Youthful, truthful Lucy "X,"
Let her know she's better than she suspects.
Now if you see Jessie "Y,"

Faded, jaded Jessie "Y,"
Tell her that she's sweller than apple pie.
Juicy Lucy,
Dressy Jessie,
Tell them that they ought to get together quick,
'Cause getting it together is the whole trick!

A LITTLE NIGHT MUSIC

Now

FREDRIK

Now,
As the sweet imbecilities
Tumble so lavishly
Onto her lap . . .
Now,
There are two possibilities:
A, I could ravish her,
B, I could nap . . .

Say
It's the ravishment, then we see
The option
That follows, of course:
A,
The deployment of charm, or B,
The adoption
Of physical force . . .

Now B might arouse her,
But let us assume
I trip on my trouser
Leg crossing the room . . .
Her hair getting tangled,
Her stays getting snapped,

My nerves would be jangled,
My energy sapped . . .

Removing her clothing
Would take me all day
And her subsequent loathing
Would turn me away,
Which eliminates B
And which leaves us with A . . .

Now,
Insofar as approaching it,
What would be festive
But have its effect? . . .
Now,
There are two ways of broaching it:
A, the suggestive
And B, the direct . . .

Say
That I settle on B, to wit,
A charmingly
Lecherous mood . . .
A,
I could put on my nightshirt or sit
Disarmingly,
B, in the nude . . .

That might be effective,
My body's all right,

But not in perspective
And not in the light . . .

I'm bound to be chilly
And feel a buffoon,
But nightshirts are silly
In mid-afternoon . . .

Which leaves the suggestive,
But how to proceed?
Although she gets restive,
Perhaps I could read . . .

In view of her penchant
For something romantic,
De Sade is too trenchant
And Dickens too frantic,
And Stendhal would ruin
The plan of attack,
As there isn't much blue in
The Red and The Black.

De Maupassant's candor
Would cause her dismay.
The Brontës are grander,
But not very gay.
Her taste is much blander,
I'm sorry to say,
But is Hans Christian Ander-
Sen ever risqué?

Which eliminates A . . .

Now,
With my mental facilities
Partially muddied
And ready to snap . . .
Now,
Though there are possibilities
Still to be studied,
I might as well nap . . .

Bow
Though I must
To adjust
My original plan . . .
How
Shall I sleep
Half as deep
As I usually can? . . .

When now I still want and/or love you,
Now as always,
Now,
Anne . . .

Soon

Soon, I promise.
Soon I won't shy away,
Dear old—

(*Catches herself*)

Soon. I want to.
Soon, whatever you say.

Even now,
When you're close and we touch
And you're kissing my brow,
I don't mind it too much.
And you'll have to admit
I'm endearing,
I help keep things humming,
I'm not domineering,
What's one small shortcoming?
And think of how I adore you,
Think of how much you love me.
If I were perfect for you,
Wouldn't you tire of me
Soon,
All too soon,
Dear old—?
Soon—

HENRIK
"Later" . . .

ANNE
I promise.

HENRIK
When is "Later"?

ANNE	HENRIK
Soon	"Later, Henrik, later."
I won't shy	All you ever hear is,
Away,	"Yes, we know, Henrik,
	Oh Henrik,
	Everyone agrees, Henrik,

ANNE	HENRIK	FREDRIK
Dear Old . . .	Please, Henrik!"	
Soon.		(*In his sleep*)
	"Later" . . .	Now,
		As the
I want to.	When is "later"?	Sweet imbecilities
	All you ever hear is	
Soon,		Trip on my
	"Later,	Trouser leg,
Whatever you	Henrik,	Stendhal
	Later."	
	As I've often	Eliminates

ANNE	HENRIK	FREDRIK
Say,	Stated:	"A," But
	When?	When?
Even	Maybe	Maybe
Now,	Soon,	Later.
When you're		
Close and we	Soon,	
Touch,	I'll be	
	Ninety and	
And you're		When I'm
Kissing my	Dead.	Kissing your
Brow,		Brow and I'm
		Stroking your
		Head,
I don't mind it	I don't mind it	You'll come
Too much,	Too much,	Into my bed.
And you'll	Since I	And you'll
Have to admit	Have to admit I	Have to admit
I'm		I've
Endearing, I	Find peering	Been hearing
Help keep	Through life's gray	All those
Things		Tremulous
Humming,	Windows	Cries
	Impatiently	
I'm not	Not	Patiently, not
Domineering,	Very cheering.	
What's		Interfering
One small	Do I fear	With those
Short-		Tremulous
Coming?	Death? Let it	Thighs

84

ANNE	HENRIK	FREDRIK
And	Come to me	Come to me
Think of how	Now,	Soon,
I adore you,		
Think of how	Now,	Soon,
Much you love		
Me.		
If I were	Now,	Soon,
Perfect		
For you,		
Wouldn't you	Now.	Soon.
Tire of me		
Later?	Come to me	Come to me
	Soon. If I'm	Soon,
We will,	Dead, I can	
Later.	Wait.	Straight to me,
	How can I	Never mind how.
We will . . .	Live until	Darling.
Soon,	Later?	Now
		I still want
		And/or
	Later . . .	Love you.
Soon,		
		Now as
	Later . . .	Always,
Soon.		
		Now,
		Desiree

       FREDRIK

   Desiree . . .

Later

HENRIK

Later . . .
When is later? . . .
All you ever hear is, "Later, Henrik—
Henrik, Later . . ."

"Yes, we know, Henrik,
Oh, Henrik,
Everyone agrees, Henrik,
Please, Henrik!"

You have a thought you're fairly bursting with,
A personal discovery or problem, and it's
"What's your rush, Henrik?
Shush, Henrik,
Goodness, how you gush, Henrik,
Hush, Henrik!"

You murmur,
"I only—
It's just that—
For God's sake—!"
"Later, Henrik . . ."

"Henrik" . . .
Who is "Henrik"?
"Oh, that lawyer's son, the one who mumbles,
Short and boring.

Yes, he's hardly worth ignoring."
And who cares if he's all dammed—
I beg your pardon—
Up inside?

As I've often stated,
It's intolerable
Being tolerated.
"Reassure Henrik,
Poor Henrik.
Henrik, you'll endure
Being pure, Henrik."

Though I've been born, I've never been!
How can I wait around for later?
I'll be ninety on my deathbed
And the late, or rather later,
Henrik Egerman!

Doesn't anything begin?

The Miller's Son

PETRA

I shall marry the miller's son
Pin my hat on a nice piece of property.
Friday nights, for a bit of fun,
We'll go dancing.
Meanwhile . . .

It's a wink and a wiggle
And a giggle on the grass
And I'll trip the light fandango,
A pinch and a diddle
In the middle of what pass-
Es by.

It's a very short road
From the pinch and the punch
To the paunch and the pouch
And the pension.
It's a very short road
To the ten-thousandth lunch
And the belch and the grouch
And the sigh.

In the meanwhile,
There are mouths to be kissed
Before mouths to be fed,
And a lot in between
In the meanwhile.

And a girl ought to celebrate
What passes by.

Or I shall marry the businessman:
Five fat babies and lots of security.
Friday nights, if we think we can,
We'll go dancing.
Meanwhile . . .

It's a push and a fumble
And a tumble in the sheets
And I'll foot the Highland Fancy,
A dip in the butter
And a flutter with what meets
My eye.

It's a very short fetch
From the push and the whoop
To the squint and the stoop
And the mumble.
It's not much of a stretch
To the cribs and the croup
And the bosoms that droop
And go dry.

In the meanwhile,
There are mouths to be kissed
Before mouths to be fed,
And there's many a tryst
And there's many a bed

To be sampled and seen
In the meanwhile.
And a girl has to celebrate
What passes by.

Or I shall marry the Prince of Wales:
Pearls and servants and dressing for festivals.
Friday nights, with him all in tails,
We'll have dancing.
Meanwhile . . .

It's a rip in the bustle
And a rustle in the hay
And I'll pitch the Quick Fantastic,
With flings of confetti
And my petticoats away
Up high.

It's a very short way
From the fling that's for fun
To the thigh pressing un-
Der the table.
It's a very short day
Till you're stuck with just one
Or it has to be done
On the sly.

In the meanwhile,
There are mouths to be kissed
Before mouths to be fed,

And there's many a tryst
And there's many a bed.
There's a lot I'll have missed,
But I'll not have been dead
When I die!
And a person should celebrate
Everything passing by.

And I shall marry the miller's son.

Send in the Clowns

DESIREE
Isn't it rich?
Are we a pair?
Me here at last on the ground,
You in mid-air.
Send in the clowns.

Isn't it bliss?
Don't you approve?
One who keeps tearing around,
One who can't move.
Where are the clowns?
Send in the clowns.

Just when I'd stopped opening doors,
Finally knowing the one that I wanted
   was yours,
Making my entrance again with my usual flair,
Sure of my lines,
No one is there.

Don't you love farce?
My fault, I fear.
I thought that you'd want what I want.
Sorry, my dear.
But where are the clowns?
Quick, send in the clowns.
Don't bother, they're here.

Isn't it rich?
Isn't it queer,
Losing my timing this late
In my career?
And where are the clowns?
There ought to be clowns.
Well, maybe next year . . .

Every Day a Little Death

CHARLOTTE

Every day a little death,
In the parlor, in the bed,
In the curtains, in the silver,
In the buttons, in the bread.
Every day a little sting
In the heart and in the head.
Every move and every breath,
And you hardly feel a thing,
Brings a perfect little death.

He smiles sweetly, strokes my hair,
Says he misses me.
I would murder him right there,
But first I die.

He talks softly of his wars
And his horses and his whores.
I think love's a dirty business!

ANNE

So do I! So do I . . .

CHARLOTTE

I'm before him on my knees
And he kisses me.
He assumes I'll lose my reason,
And I do.

Men are stupid, men are vain,
Love's disgusting, love's insane,
A humiliating business!

ANNE
Oh, how true!

CHARLOTTE
Ah, well . . .

Every day a little death—

ANNE
Every day a little death—

CHARLOTTE
In the parlor, in the bed—

ANNE
On the lips and in the eyes—

CHARLOTTE	ANNE
In the curtains,	In the murmurs,
In the silver,	In the pauses,
In the buttons,	In the gestures,
In the bread.	In the sighs.
Every day a	
Little sting	
	Every day a little dies
In the heart	
And in the head.	In the looks
	And in the lies.

Every move and every breath—

And you hardly feel a thing,
Brings a perfect little death.

Remember?

QUINTET

(*Individually*)

The old deserted beach that we walked—
Remember?
The café in the park where we talked—
Remember?
The tenor on the boat that we chartered,
Belching "The Bartered Bride"—
Ah, how we laughed,
Ah, how we cried.
Ah, how you promised,
And ah, how I lied.

That dilapidated inn—
Remember, darling?
The proprietress' grin,
Also her glare.
Yellow gingham on the bed—
Remember, darling?
And the canopy in red,
Needing repair?

I *think* you were there . . .

The local village dance on the green—
Remember?

The lady with the large tambourine—
Remember?

The one who played the harp in her boa
Thought she was so a-
Dept.
Ah, how we laughed,
Ah, how we wept.
Ah, how we polka'd and ah,
How we slept.

How we kissed and how we clung—
Remember, darling?
We were foolish, we were young—
More than we knew.
Yellow gingham on the bed,
Remember, darling?
And the canopy in red,
Or was it blue?

The funny little games that we played—
Remember?
The unexpected knock of the maid—
Remember?
The wine that made us both rather merry
And, oh, so very
Frank.
Ah, how we laughed,
Ah, how we drank.

You acquiesced and the rest
Is a blank.

What we did with your perfume—
Remember, darling?
The condition of the room
When we were through . . .
Our inventions were unique—
Remember, darling?
I was limping for a week,
You caught the flu.

I'm *sure* it was—
You . . .

Liaisons

MADAME ARMFELDT

At the villa of the Baron De Signac,
Where I spent a somewhat infamous year,
At the villa of the Baron De Signac
I had ladies in attendance,
Fire-opal pendants . . .

Liaisons! What's happened to them,
Liaisons today?
Disgraceful! What's become of them?
Some of them
Hardly pay their shoddy way.

What once was a rare Champagne
Is now just an amiable hock,
What once was a villa, at least,
Is "digs."
What once was a gown with train
Is now just a simple little frock,
What once was a sumptuous feast
Is figs.
No, not even figs—
Raisins.
Ah, liaisons!

Where was I? . . . Oh, yes . . .

At the palace of the Duke of Ferrara,
Who was prematurely deaf but a dear,
At the palace of the Duke of Ferrara,
I acquired some position,
Plus a tiny Titian . . .

Liaisons! What's happened to them,
Liaisons today?
To see them – indiscriminate
Women, it
Pains me more than I can say,
The lack of taste that they display.

Where is style?
Where is skill?
Where is forethought?
Where's discretion of the heart,
Where's passion in the art,
Where's craft?
With a smile
And a will
But with more thought,
I acquired a château
Extravagantly o-
Verstaffed.

Too many people muddle sex
With mere desire,

And when emotion intervenes,
The nets descend.
It should on no account perplex,
Or worse, inspire.
It's but a pleasurable means
To a measurable end.
Why does no one comprehend?
Let us hope this lunacy is just a trend.

    Where was I? . . . Oh, yes . . .

In the castle of the King of the Belgians,
We would visit through a false chiffonier,
In the castle of the King of the Belgians,
Who, when things got rather touchy,
Deeded me a duchy . . .

Liaisons! What's happened to them,
Liaisons today?
Untidy – take my daughter, I
Taught her, I
Tried my best to point the way.
I even named her Desiree.

In a world where the kings are employers,
Where the amateur prevails
And delicacy fails
To pay,
In a world where the princes are lawyers,
What can anyone expect

Except to recollect
Liai . . .

(*She falls asleep*)

THE FROGS

Paean: Hades

PLUTO

Everybody dumps on Hades,
People yelling, "Go to Hell!"
Well,
Let me tell you, life in Hades
Is just swell!

It's got flash! It's got flair!
It's got spectacle to spare!
People come from everywhere,
Like it or not—
Mostly not.
Then they see what we've got
And they like it a lot.
Hell is hot.

I mean,
You never gain weight,
You're never out-of-date,
You never get balder, older,
You never have to fret about Fate,
It's all too late—
I mean, you're dead.

You're not afraid of time rushing by.
Not afraid of oceans running dry,

All because you're not afraid to die,
Once you're dead.

And you get to live in Hades,
Where it's always two a.m.,
Where it's party till you drop
And never stop,
Because there's nothing we condemn.
Where whatever you regret
You just forget,
Or better yet,
Forgive.
Where you're not afraid to die,
And when you're not afraid to die,
Then you're not afraid to live!

And you're living here in Hades,
And I mean you're living well.
Everybody comes to Hades.
Everybody goes to Hell.

Up there, lots of sun,
Down here, fire and gloom.
Up there, not a lot of fun,
Down here, va-va-voom!
Up there, gotta get a grip.
Down here, one long acid trip.
R.I.P. down here means "Let 'er rip!"
Hell is hot,

Hell is happening,
Hell is cool!

Up there, that's just life.
Down here, this is living,
An endless party that no one's giving,
But everybody's invited.

Once you settle down in Hades,
You can leave the world behind.
Here where everyone is gay—
No, not that way—
No, I mean *gay*—
Oh, never mind.

Everyone's afraid of Hades,
So they never misbehave.
If they got a glimpse of Hades,
They'd be racing to the grave.

Here no one has a need anymore
To commit a murder, wage a war.
Who're you going to murder, and what for?
They're all like dead.

ALL
Deceased,
Kaput, defunct, released . . .

PLUTO
And we're flying high in Hades,

Where it's always two a.m.,
Where it's party till you drop
And never stop,
Because there's nothing we condemn!

GIRLS
For the mortal human race
Who need their space,
This is the place
To be.

PLUTO
'Cause you're not afraid of death,
And when you're not afraid of death,
Then you're ready for *la vie*!

GIRLS
Day is night when you're in Hades.

PLUTO
That's the thing that gives it zing!
How about a hand for Hades?

GIRLS
Ooh ooh ooh ooh ooh ooh . . .

PLUTO
I just love being king.

ALL
Hail to Pluto!

All Aboard!

CHARON

All aboard!
Hades express!
Nonstop,
Just a short hop
To the bottomless pit—
This is it!

All aboard!
Club Dead
Straight ahead!
Bring your shroud,
No coffins allowed—
There's too big a crowd.

But if you're a stiff,
Then get in the skiff
And we're off to perdition.
And wait till you see perdition:

You think you know dank?
Hoo, boy.
You think you know dismal?
Sheesh, forget it.
Talk about dark,
Talk about dreary,

What you think is dreary
Is what we call cheery
Down here on the River Styx.

All aboard!
No delay,
Long as you're D.O.A.

If you fell off of the perch,
If you bought the farm,
Kicked the bucket,
Bit the dust,
All aboard!
You're going down
To that toddling town—
And I do mean *down* . . .

PACIFIC OVERTURES

Poems

KAYAMA
Rain glistening
On the silver birch,
Like my lady's tears . . .
Your turn.

MANJIRO
Rain gathering,
Winding into streams,
Like the roads to Boston . . .
Your turn.

KAYAMA
Haze hovering,
Like the whisper of the silk
As my lady kneels . . .
Your turn.

MANJIRO
Haze glittering,
Like an echo of the lamps
In the streets of Boston . . .
Your turn.

KAYAMA
Moon,
I love her like the moon,

Making jewels of the grass
Where my lady walks,
My lady wife . . .

MANJIRO
Moon,
I love her like the moon,
Washing yesterday away,
As my lady does,
America . . .
Your turn.

KAYAMA
Wind murmuring.
Is she murmuring for me
Through her field of dreams? . . .
Your turn.

MANJIRO
Wind muttering.
Is she quarreling with me?
Does she want me home? . . .
Your turn.

KAYAMA
I am no nightingale,
But she hears the song
I can sing to her,
My lady wife . . .

MANJIRO

I am no nightingale,
But my song of her
Could outsing the sea . . .
America . . .

KAYAMA

Dawn flickering,
Tracing shadows of the pines
On my lady sleeping . . .
Your turn.

MANJIRO

Dawn brightening
As she opens up her eyes
But it's I who come awake . . .
Your turn.

KAYAMA

You go.

MANJIRO

Your turn.

BOTH

Leaves,
I love her like the leaves,
Changing green to pink gold,
And the change is everything.

Sun,
I see her like the sun

In the center of a pool,
Sending ripples to the shore,
Till my journey's end.

    MANJIRO
Your turn.

    KAYAMA
Rain . . .

    MANJIRO
Haze . . .

    KAYAMA
Moon . . .

    MANJIRO
Wind . . .

    KAYAMA
Nightingale . . .

    MANJIRO
Dawn . . .

    KAYAMA
Leaves . . .

    MANJIRO
Sun . . .

    BOTH
End.

A Bowler Hat

KAYAMA

It's called a bowler hat.
I have no wife.
The swallow flying through the sky
Is not as swift as I
Am, flying through my life.
You pour the milk before the tea.
The Dutch ambassador is no fool.
I must remember that.

I wear a bowler hat.
They send me wine.
The house is far too grand.
I've bought a new umbrella stand.
Today I visited the church beside the shrine.
I'm learning English from a book.
Most exciting.
It's called a bowler hat.

It's called a pocket watch.
I have a wife.
No eagle flies against the sky
As eagerly as I
Have flown against my life.
One smokes American cigars.
The Dutch ambassador was most rude.
I will remember that.

I wind my pocket watch.
We serve white wine.
The house is far too small.
I killed a spider on the wall.
One of the servants thought it was a lucky sign.
I read Spinoza every day.
Formidable.
Where is my bowler hat?

It's called a monocle.
I've left my wife.
No bird exploring in the sky
Explores as well as I
The corners of my life.
One must keep moving with the times.
The Dutch ambassador is a fool.
He wears a bowler hat.

They call them spectacles.
I drink much wine.
I take imported pills.
I have a house up in the hills
I've hired British architects to redesign.
One must accommodate the times
As one lives them.
One must remember that.

It's called a cutaway . . .

SWEENEY TODD

A Little Priest

MRS. LOVETT
Seems a downright shame . . .
Seems an awful waste . . .
Such a nice plump frame
Wot's-his-name
Has . . .
Had . . .
Has . . .
Nor it can't be traced.

Business needs a lift,
Debts to be erased.
Think of it as thrift,
As a gift . . .
If you get my drift . . .
No?
Seems an awful waste.

I mean,
With the price of meat what it is,
When you get it,
If you get it—

TODD
Ah!

MRS. LOVETT
Good, you got it.

Take, for instance,
Mrs. Mooney and her pie shop:
Business never better, using only pussy cats
    and toast.
And a pussy's good for maybe six or seven
    at the most.
And I'm sure they can't compare as far
    as taste . . .

TODD	MRS. LOVETT
Mrs. Lovett,	
What a charming notion,	
Eminently practical and	Well, it
yet	does seem a
Appropriate, as always.	Waste . . .
Mrs. Lovett, how	
I've lived	
Without you all	It's an idea . . .
these years	
I'll never know!	Think about it . . .
How delectable!	Lots of other
	gentlemen'll
Also undetectable.	Soon be coming for
	a shave,
	Won't they?
	Think of

How choice!   All them
How rare!   Pies!

TODD

For what's the sound of the world out there?

MRS. LOVETT

What, Mr. Todd, what, Mr. Todd,
What is that sound?

TODD

Those crunching noises pervading the air?

MRS. LOVETT

Yes, Mr. Todd, yes, Mr. Todd,
Yes, all around.

TODD

It's man devouring man, my dear—

BOTH

And who are we to deny it in here?

TODD

These are desperate times, Mrs. Lovett, and
desperate measures are called for.

MRS. LOVETT

(*Proffering an imaginary meat pie*)
Here we are, hot from the oven.

118

TODD
What is that?

MRS. LOVETT
It's priest.
Have a little priest.

TODD
Is it really good?

MRS. LOVETT
Sir, it's too good, at least.
Then again, they don't commit sins of the flesh,
So it's pretty fresh.

TODD
Awful lot of fat.

MRS. LOVETT
Only where it sat.

TODD
Haven't you got poet
Or something like that?

MRS. LOVETT
No, you see the trouble with poet
Is how do you know it's
Deceased?
Try the priest.

TODD

(*Pretending to taste it*)

Heavenly. Not as hearty as bishop, perhaps, but not as bland as curate, either.

MRS. LOVETT

And good for business – always leaves you wanting more. Trouble is, we only get it in Sundays . . .

Lawyer's rather nice.

TODD

If it's for a price.

MRS. LOVETT

Order something else, though, to follow,
Since no one should swallow
It twice.

TODD

Anything that's lean.

MRS. LOVETT

Well, then, if you're British and loyal,
You might enjoy Royal
Marine.
Anyway, it's clean.
Though, of course, it tastes of wherever it's been.

TODD
Is that squire
On the fire?

MRS. LOVETT
Mercy, no, sir,
Look closer,
You'll notice it's grocer.

TODD
Looks thicker,
More like vicar.

MRS. LOVETT
No, it has to be grocer – it's green.

TODD
The history of the world, my love . . .

MRS. LOVETT
Save a lot of graves,
Do a lot of relatives favors . . .

TODD
Is those below serving those up above.

MRS. LOVETT
Everybody shaves,
So there should be plenty of flavors . . .

TODD
How gratifying for once to know—

BOTH
(*Indicates the room upstairs*)
That those above will serve those down below!

MRS. LOVETT
Now, let me see . . .
We've got tinker.

TODD
Something pinker.

MRS. LOVETT
Tailor?

TODD
(*Pondering*)
Something – paler.

MRS. LOVETT
Butler?

TODD
Something – subtler.

MRS. LOVETT
Potter?

TODD
Something – hotter.

MRS. LOVETT
Locksmith?

(*Todd is stumped*)

Lovely bit of clerk.

    TODD
Maybe for a lark . . .

    MRS. LOVETT
Then again, there's sweep
If you want it cheap
And you like it dark.

Try the financier—
Peak of his career.

    TODD
That looks pretty rank.

    MRS. LOVETT
Well, he drank.
It's a bank
Cashier.

Last one really sold.
Wasn't quite so old.

    TODD
Have you any beadle?

    MRS. LOVETT
Next week, so I'm told.
Beadle isn't bad till you smell it

And notice how well it's
Been greased.
Stick to priest.

TODD
The history of the world, my sweet—

MRS. LOVETT
Oh, Mr. Todd, ooh, Mr. Todd,
What does it tell?

TODD
Is who gets eaten and who gets to eat.

MRS. LOVETT
And, Mr. Todd, too, Mr. Todd,
Who gets to sell.

TODD
But fortunately, it's also clear—

BOTH
That (But) everybody
Goes down well with beer.

TODD
(*As she proffers another pie*)
What is that?

MRS. LOVETT
It's fop.
Finest in the shop.

And we have some shepherd's pie peppered
With actual shepherd
On top.
And I've just begun.
Here's the politician: so oily
It's served with a doily—
Not one?

TODD
Put it on a bun.

(*As she looks at him quizzically*)

Well, you never know if it's going to run.

MRS. LOVETT
Try the friar.
Fried, it's drier.

TODD
No, the clergy is really
Too coarse and too mealy.

MRS. LOVETT
Then actor—
That's compacter.

TODD
Yes, and always arrives overdone.

I'll come again when you
Have judge on the menu . . .

Have charity toward the world, my pet.

MRS. LOVETT
Yes, yes, I know, my love.

TODD
We'll take the customers that we can get.

MRS. LOVETT
High-born and low, my love.

TODD
We'll not discriminate great from small.
No, we'll serve anyone—
Meaning anyone—

BOTH
And to anyone
At all!

Not While I'm Around

TOBIAS
Nothing's gonna harm you,
Not while I'm around.
Nothing's gonna harm you,
No, sir,
Not while I'm around.

Demons are prowling
Everywhere
Nowadays.
I'll send them howling,
I don't care—
I got ways.

No one's gonna hurt you,
No one's gonna dare.
Others can desert you—
Not to worry,
Whistle, I'll be there.

Demons'll charm you
With a smile
For a while,
But in time
Nothing can harm you,
Not while I'm
Around.

Not to worry, not to worry,
I may not be smart but I ain't dumb.
I can do it,
Put me to it,
Show me something I can overcome.
Not to worry, mum.

Being close and being clever
Ain't like being true.
I don't need to, I won't never
Hide a thing from you,
Like some.

MRS. LOVETT
Nothing's gonna harm you,
Not while I'm around!
Nothing's gonna harm you, Toby,
Not while I'm around.

TOBIAS
Two quid was in it,
Two or three—
    The guv'nor giving up his purse—
    with two quid?

Not for a minute!
Don't you see? . . .

Demons'll charm you
With a smile

For a while,
But in time
Nothing's gonna harm you,
Not while I'm
Around!

MARRY ME A LITTLE

Uptown/Downtown

PHYLLIS

Now this is the tale of a dame
Known as Harriet,
Who climbed to the top of the heap
   from the bottom.
A beautiful life was her aim,
And to vary it
She wanted the sun and the moon,
   and she got 'em.
She isn't the least exhausted from her climb,
But she does look back from time to time,
And the subject of this evening's quiz
Is who she was, and who she is:

Uptown, she's stepping out with a swell.
Downtown, she's holding hands on the El—
Hyphenated Harriet,
The nouveau
From New Ro-
Chelle.

Uptown, she's got the Vanderbilt clans.
Downtown, she's with the sidewalk Cézannes—
Hyphenated Harriet,
The nouveau

From New Ro-
Chelle.

She sits
At the Ritz
With her splits
Of Mumm's
And starts to pine
For a stein
With her village chums,
But with a Schlitz
In her mitts
Down in Fitz-
Roy's Bar,
She thinks of the Ritz – oh,
It's so
Schizo.

Uptown, it's Harry Winston she needs.
Downtown, its strictly zircons and beads.
Ask her, should she be Uptown or Down?
She's two of the most miserable girls in town.

MERRILY WE ROLL ALONG

Like It Was

> MARY

Hey, old friend,
What do you say, old friend?
Make it okay, old friend,
Give the old friendship a break.
Why so grim?
We're going on forever.
You, me, him,
Too many lives are at stake.

Friends this long
Has to mean something's strong,
So if our old friend's wrong,
Shouldn't an old friend come through?
It's us, old friend—
What's to discuss, old friend?
Here's to us,
Who's like us—?

> CHARLEY

Damn few.

> MARY

Charley,

Why can't it be like it was?
I liked it the way that it was.
Charley,
You and me, we were nicer then.

We were nice,
Kids and cities and trees were nice,
Everything . . .
I don't know who we are anymore,
And I'm starting not to care.

Look at us, Charley,
Nothing's the way that it was.
I want it the way that it was.
Help me stop remembering then.

Don't you remember?
It was good, it was really good.
Help me out, Charley,
Make it like it was.

Charley,
Nothing's the way that it was.
I want it the way that it was.
God knows, things were easier then.

Trouble is, Charley,
That's what everyone does:
Blames the way it is
On the way it was.
On the way it never ever was . . .

Not a Day Goes By
(*Reprise*)

BETH

Not a day goes by . . .

MARY

Not a single day . . .

MARY, BETH

But you're somewhere a part of my life
And it looks like you'll stay.

FRANK, MARY

As the days go by,
I keep thinking, when does it end?

BETH

That it can't get much better much longer.
But it only gets better and stronger
And deeper and nearer—

FRANK, BETH

And simple and freer
And richer and clearer . . .

ALL THREE

And no,
Not a day goes by—

MARY

Not a blessed day—

BETH, MARY
But you somewhere come into my life
And you don't go away.

ALL THREE
And I have to say
If you do, I'll die.

FRANK, BETH
I want day after day
After day after day after—

MARY
(*Overlapping*)
I'll die day after day after—

ALL THREE
Day after day after day after day
After day,
Till the days go by . . .

FRANK, BETH
Till the days go by . . .

MARY
Till the days go by . . .

Not a Day Goes By

BETH

Not a day goes by,
Not a single day
But you're somewhere a part of my life,
And it looks like you'll stay.

As the days go by,
I keep thinking, when does it end?
Where's the day I'll have started forgetting?

(*With increasing fury*)

But I just go on
Thinking and sweating
And cursing and crying
And turning and reaching
And waking and dying
And no,
Not a day goes by,
Not a blessed day
But you're still somehow part of my life,
And you won't go away.

So there's hell to pay,
And until I die,
I'll die day after day
After day after day

After day after day
After day,
Till the days go by!
Till the days go by!
Till the days go by!

SUNDAY IN THE PARK
WITH GEORGE

Sunday in the Park with George

DOT
A trickle of sweat
The back of the head
He always does this
Now the foot is dead
Sunday in the park with George
One more Sun—
The collar is damp
Beginning to pinch
The bustle's slipping
I won't budge one inch
Who was at the zoo, George?
Who was at the zoo?
The monkeys and who, George?
The monkeys and who?

GEORGE
Don't move.

DOT
Artists are bizarre. Fixed. Cold
That's you, George,
You're bizarre. Fixed. Cold
I like that in a man

Fixed. Cold.
God, it's hot up here

Well, there are worse things
Than staring at the water on a Sunday
There are worse things
Than staring at the water
As you're posing for a picture
Being painted by your lover
In the middle of the summer
On an island in the river on a Sunday

The petticoat's wet
Which adds to the weight
The sun is blinding
All right, concentrate

GEORGE
Eyes open please

DOT
Sunday in the park with George

GEORGE
Look out at the water, not at me

DOT
Sunday in the park with George

Well, if you want bread
And respect

And attention
Not to say connection
Modeling's no profession

If you want instead when you're dead
Some more public and more permanent
    expression
Of affection
You want a painter, poet, sculptor
    preferably
Marble, granite, bronze
Durable
Something nice with swans
That's durable forever
All it has to be is good
And George, you're good
You're really good

George's stroke is tender
George's touch is pure

Your eyes, George
I love your eyes, George
I love your beard, George
I love your size, George
But most, George, of all
But most of all
I love your painting . . .
I think I'm fainting

The tip of a stay
Right under the tit
No, don't give in
Just lift the arm a bit

GEORGE
Don't lift the arm, please

DOT
Sunday in the park with George

The bustle high, please
Not even a nod
As if I were trees
The ground could open
He would still say "please"

Never know with you, George,
Who could know with you?
The others I knew, George.
Before we get through,
I'll get to you, too.
God I am so hot

Well, there are worse things
Than staring at the water on a Sunday.
There are worse things
Than staring at the water
As you're posing for a picture
After sleeping on the ferry

After getting up at seven
To come over to an island
In the middle of a river
Half an hour from the city
On a Sunday
On a Sunday in the park with . . .

    GEORGE
Don't move the mouth

    DOT
George!

Everybody Loves Louis

DOT

Hello, George . . .
Where did you go, George?
I know you're near, George.
I caught your eyes, George.
I want your ear, George.
I've a surprise, George . . .

Everybody loves Louis,
Louis's simple and kind.
Everybody loves Louis,
Louis's lovable.

Seems we never know, do we,
Who we're going to find?
And Louis the baker—
Is not what I had in mind.
But . . .

Louis's really an artist:
Louis's cakes are an art.
Louis isn't the smartest—
Louis's popular.
Everybody loves Louis:
Louis bakes from the heart . . .

The bread, George.
I mean the bread, George.
And then in bed, George . . .

I mean he kneads me—
I mean like dough, George . . .
Hello, George . . .

Louis's always so pleasant,
Louis's always so fair.
Louis makes you feel present,
Louis's generous.
That's the thing about Louis:
Louis always is *there.*
Louis's thoughts are not hard to follow,
Louis's art is not hard to swallow.

Not that Louis's perfection—
That's what makes him ideal.
Hardly anything worth objection:
Louis drinks a bit,
Louis blinks a bit.
Louis makes a connection,
That's the thing that you feel . . .

We lose things.
And then we choose things.
And there are Louis's.
And there are Georges—
Well, Louis's
And George.

But George has George,
And I need someone—
Louis . . .

Beautiful

OLD LADY

Changing.
It keeps changing.
I see towers
Where there were trees.

Going,
All the stillness,
The solitude,
Georgie.

Sundays
Disappearing
All the time,
When things were beautiful . . .

GEORGE

All things are beautiful,
Mother,
All trees, all towers,
Beautiful.
That tower—
Beautiful, Mother,
See?

(*Gestures*)

A perfect tree.

Pretty isn't beautiful, Mother,
Pretty is what changes.
What the eye arranges
Is what is beautiful.

OLD LADY
Fading . . .

GEORGE
I'm changing.
You're changing.

OLD LADY
It keeps fading . . .

GEORGE
I'll draw us now before we fade,
Mother.

OLD LADY
It keeps melting before our eyes.

GEORGE
You watch
While I revise the world.

OLD LADY
Changing,
As we sit here—
Quick, draw it all, Georgie!

BOTH
Sundays—

OLD LADY
Disappearing,
As we look.

GEORGE
Look! . . .
Look! . . .

OLD LADY
(*Not listening, fondly*)
You make it beautiful.

Sunday

Sunday,
By the blue
Purple yellow red water
On the green
Purple yellow red grass,
Let us pass
Through our perfect park,

Pausing on a Sunday
By the cool
Blue triangular water
On the soft
Green elliptical grass,
As we pass
Through arrangements of shadows
Toward the verticals of trees
Forever . . .

By the blue
Purple yellow red water
On the green
Orange violet mass
Of the grass
In our perfect park,

GEORGE
Made of flecks of light
And dark,

MEN
And parasols . . .

GEORGE
Bumbum bum bumbumbum
Bumbum bum . . .

ALL
People strolling through the trees
Of a small suburban park
On an island in the river
On an ordinary Sunday . . .

Sunday . . .

Sunday . . .

Finishing the Hat

GEORGE

Yes, she looks for me.
Good.
Let her look for me to tell me why she left me—
As I always knew she would.
I had thought she understood.
They have never understood,
And no reason that they should,
But if anybody could . . .

Finishing the hat,
How you have to finish the hat,
How you watch the rest of the world
From a window
While you finish the hat.

Mapping out a sky,
What you feel like, planning a sky,
What you feel when voices that come
Through the window
Go
Until they distance and die,
Until there's nothing but sky.

And how you're always turning back too late
From the grass or the stick
Or the dog or the light,
How the kind of woman willing to wait's

150

Not the kind that you want to find waiting
To return you to the night,
Dizzy from the height,
Coming from the hat,

Studying the hat,
Entering the world of the hat,
Reaching through the world of the hat
Like a window,
Back to this one from that.

Studying a face,
Stepping back to look at a face
Leaves a little space in the way like a window,
But to see—
It's the only way to see.

And when the woman that you wanted goes,
You can say to yourself, "Well, I give what
     I give."
But the woman who won't wait for you knows
That however you live,
There's a part of you always standing by,
Mapping out the sky,
Finishing a hat,
Starting on a hat,
Finishing a hat . . .

Look, I made a hat
Where there never was a hat.

Putting It Together
(*Barbra Streisand version*)

BARBRA

(*To herself*)
Be nice, girl.
You have to pay a price, girl.
They like to give advice, girl.
Don't think about it twice, girl.
It's time to get to work.

Art isn't easy
Even when you're hot.
Advancing art is easy,
Financing it is not.

A vision's just a vision
If it's only in your head.
If no one gets to share it,
It's as good as dead.
It has to come to life!

Bit by bit,
Putting it together . . . etc. . . . .

Ounce by ounce,
Putting it together . . . etc. . . . .

Link by link,
Making the connections.
Drink by drink,

Taking every comment as it comes.
Learning how to play the politician
Like you play piano, bass and drums.
Otherwise you'll find your composition
Isn't gonna get an exhibition.

Art isn't easy.
Every minor detail is a major decision . . . etc. . . .
. . . Every time I start to feel defensive,
I remember vinyl is expensive . . . etc. . . .

Dot by dot
Building up the image . . . etc. . . .
. . . Even when you get some recognition,
Everything you do, you still audition . . . etc. . . .
. . . All they really want is repetition,
All they really like is what they know.
Gotta keep a link with your tradition,
Gotta learn to trust your intuition,
While you re-establish your position
So that you can be on exhibit—

So that your *work* can be on exhibition!

Be new, girl.
They tell you till they're blue, girl.
You're new or else you're through, girl.
And even if it's true, girl.
You do what you can do!

Bit by bit,
Putting it together . . . etc. . . .

The record executives argue about her, as in the
original: "She's an original." "Was!" and so forth.

Mapping out the songs, but in addition
Harmonizing each negotiation,
Balancing the part that's all musician
With the part that's strictly preparation,
Balancing the money with the mission
Till you have the perfect orchestration,
Even if you do have the suspicion
That it's taking all your concentration.
The art of making art
Is putting it together—

Bit by bit,
Beat by beat,
Part by part,
Phrase by phrase,
Chart by chart,

(*Her voices overlapping*)

Track by track,	Take by take,
Reel by reel,	Break by break,
Snack by snack,	Snit by snit,
Deal by deal,	Fit by fit,

| Shout by shout, | Hit by hit, |
| Doubt by doubt, | Bit by bit, |

(*In unison*)

And that
Is the state of the art!

Children and Art

MARIE

You would have liked him,
Mama, you would.
Mama, he makes things.
Mama, they're good.
Just as you said from the start:
Children and art . . .
Children and art . . .

He should be happy.
Mama, he's blue.
What do I do?
You should have seen it,
It was a sight.
Mama, I mean it—
All color and light!

I don't understand what it was,
But, Mama, the things that he does—!
They twinkle and shimmer and buzz.
You would have liked them . . .
It . . .
Him . . .

(*To George*)

Isn't she beautiful? There she is—

(*Pointing to different figures*)

There she is, there she is, there she is.
Mama is everywhere,
He must have loved her so much . . .

This is our family, this is the lot.
After I go, this is all that you've got,
Honey.
Wasn't she beautiful, though?

You would have liked her.
Mama did things
No one had done.
Mama was funny,
Mama was fun.
Mama spent money
When she had none.

Mama said, "Honey,
Mustn't be blue.
It's not so much do what you like
As it is that you like what you do."
Mama said, "Darling,
Don't make such a drama.
A little less thinking,
A little more feeling—"

I'm just quoting Mama . . .

(*Indicating Louise in the painting*)

The child is so sweet

(*Indicating the Celestes*)

And the girls are so rapturous.
Isn't it lovely how artists can capture us?

You would have liked her—
Honey, I'm wrong,
You would have loved her.
Mama enjoyed things.
Mama was smart.
See how she shimmers—
I mean from the heart.

I know, honey, you disagree,

(*Indicating the entire painting*)

But this is our family tree.
Just wait till we're there, and you'll see—
Listen to me . . .

(*Drifting off*)

Mama was smart . . .
Listen to Mama . . .
Children and art . . .
Children and art . . .

Move On

GEORGE
I've nothing to say.
Well, nothing that's not been said.

DOT
Said by you, though, George . . .

GEORGE
I do not know where to go.

DOT
And nor did I.

GEORGE
I want to make things that count,
Things that will be new . . .

DOT
I did what I had to do:

GEORGE
What am I to do?

DOT
Move on.

Stop worrying where you're going—
Move on.
If you can know where you're going,
You've gone.
Just keep moving on.

I chose, and my world was shaken—
So what?
The choice may have been mistaken,
The choosing was not.
You have to move on.
Look at what you want,
Not at where you are,
Not at what you'll be.
Look at all the things you've done for me:
Opened up my eyes,
Taught me how to see,
Notice every tree—

GEORGE

Notice every tree . . .

DOT

Understand the light—

GEORGE

Understand the light . . .

DOT

Concentrate on now—

GEORGE

I want to move on.
I want to explore the light.
I want to know how to get through,
Through to something new,
Something of my own—

BOTH

Move on. Move on.

DOT

Stop worrying if your vision
Is new.
Let others make that decision—
They usually do,
You keep moving on.

DOT

Look at what you've done,
Then at what you want,
Not at where you are,
What you'll be.
Look at all the things
You gave to me.

Let me give to you
Something in return.
I would be so pleased . . .

GEORGE

(*Looking around*)
Something in the light,
Something in the sky,
In the grass,
Up behind the trees . . .

Things I hadn't looked at
Till now:
Flower in your hat.
And your smile.

GEORGE

And the color of your hair,
And the way you catch the light.
And the care,
And the feeling.
And the life
Moving on!

DOT

We've always belonged together!

BOTH

We will always belong together!

DOT

Just keep moving on.

Anything you do,
Let it come from you.
Then it will be new.

Give us more to see.

INTO THE WOODS

I Know Things Now

LITTLE RED RIDING HOOD

Mother said,
"Straight ahead,"
Not to delay
Or be misled.
I should have heeded
Her advice . . .
But he seemed so nice.

And he showed me things,
Many beautiful things,
That I hadn't thought to explore.
They were off my path,
So I never had dared.
I had been so careful
I never had cared.
And he made me feel excited—
Well, excited and scared.

When he said, "Come in!"
With that sickening grin,
How could I know what was in store?
Once his teeth were bared,
Though, I really got scared—
Well, excited and scared.

But he drew me close
And he swallowed me down,
Down a dark, slimy path
Where lie secrets that I never want to know,
And when everything familiar
Seemed to disappear forever,
At the end of the path
Was Granny once again.

So we wait in the dark
Until someone sets us free,
And we're brought into the light,
And we're back at the start.

And I know things now,
Many valuable things,
That I hadn't known before:
Do not put your faith
In a cape and a hood,
They will not protect you
The way that they should.
And take extra care with strangers—
Even flowers have their dangers.
And though scary is exciting,
Nice is different than good.

Now I know:
Don't be scared.

Granny is right,
Just be prepared.
Isn't it nice to know a lot?

And a little bit not . . .

Giants in the Sky

JACK

There are giants in the sky!
There are big tall terrible giants in the sky!

When you're way up high and you look below
At the world you left and the things you know,
Little more than a glance is enough to show
You just how small you are.

When you're way up high and you're on
    your own
In a world like none that you've ever known,
Where the sky is lead and the earth is stone,

You're free to do
Whatever pleases you,
Exploring things you'd never dare
'Cause you don't care,
When suddenly there's

A big tall terrible giant at the door,
A big tall terrible lady giant sweeping the floor.
And she gives you food
And she gives you rest,
And she draws you close
To her giant breast,

And you know things now that you never
    knew before,
Not till the sky.

Only just when you've made a friend and all,
And you know she's big but you don't feel small,
Someone bigger than her comes along the hall
To swallow you for lunch.

And your heart is lead and your stomach stone
And you're really scared being all alone,
And it's then that you miss all the things
    you've known
And the world you've left and the little you own.

The fun is done.
You steal what you can and run!
And you scramble down
And you look below,
And the world you know
Begins to grow:

The roof, the house, and your mother at
    the door.
The roof, the house, and the world you never
    thought to explore.
And you think of all of the things you've seen,
And you wish that you could live in between,

And you're back again,
Only different than before,
After the sky.

There are giants in the sky!
There are big tall terrible awesome scary
Wonderful giants in the sky!

No One Is Alone

CINDERELLA
Mother cannot guide you.
Now you're on your own.
Only me beside you.
Still, you're not alone.
No one is alone, truly.
No one is alone.

Sometimes people leave you
Halfway through the wood.
Others may deceive you.
You decide what's good.
You decide alone.
But no one is alone.

CINDERELLA
(*To Little Red Riding Hood*)
Mother isn't here now.

BAKER
(*To Jack*)
Wrong things, right things . . .

CINDERELLA
Who knows what she'd say?

BAKER
Who can say what's true?

CINDERELLA

Nothing's quite so clear now.

BAKER

Do things, fight things . . .

CINDERELLA

Feel you've lost your way?

BAKER

You decide, but you are not alone.

CINDERELLA

You are not alone,
Believe me.
No one is alone.

BAKER

No one is alone,
Believe me.

CINDERELLA

Truly . . .

BAKER, CINDERELLA

You move just a finger,
Say the slightest word,
Something's bound to linger,
Be heard.

BAKER
No one acts alone.
Careful, no one is alone.

BAKER, CINDERELLA
People make mistakes.

BAKER
Fathers,

CINDERELLA
Mothers,

BAKER, CINDERELLA
People make mistakes,
Holding to their own,
Thinking they're alone.

CINDERELLA
Honor their mistakes.

BAKER
Fight for their mistakes—

CINDERELLA
Everybody makes—

BAKER, CINDERELLA
One another's
Terrible mistakes.

Witches can be right
Giants can be good.
You decide what's right,
You decide what's good.

CINDERELLA
Just remember:

BAKER
Just remember:

BAKER, CINDERELLA
Someone is on your side.

JACK, LITTLE RED RIDING HOOD
Our side.

BAKER, CINDERELLA
Our side.
Someone else is not.
While we're seeing our side—

JACK, LITTLE RED RIDING HOOD
Our side—

BAKER, CINDERELLA
Our side—

ALL FOUR
Maybe we forgot:
They are not alone.
No one is alone.

CINDERELLA
Hard to see the light now.

BAKER
Just don't let it go.

BAKER, CINDERELLA
Things will come out right now
We can make it so.
Someone is on your side—

Agony

CINDERELLA'S PRINCE
Did I abuse her
Or show her disdain?
Why does she run from me?
If I should lose her,
How shall I regain
The heart she has won from me?

Agony—!
Beyond power of speech,
When the one thing you want
Is the only thing out of your reach.

RAPUNZEL'S PRINCE
High in her tower,
She sits by the hour,
Maintaining her hair.
Blithe and becoming,
And frequently humming
A lighthearted air:

(*Hums Rapunzel's theme*)

Ah-ah-ah-ah-ah-ah-ah—

Agony—!
Far more painful than yours,

When you know she would go with you,
If there only were doors.

BOTH
Agony!
Oh, the torture they teach!

RAPUNZEL'S PRINCE
What's as intriguing—

CINDERELLA'S PRINCE
Or half so fatiguing—

BOTH
As what's out of reach?

CINDERELLA'S PRINCE
Am I not sensitive, clever,
Well-mannered, considerate,
Passionate, charming,
As kind as I'm handsome,
And heir to a throne?

RAPUNZEL'S PRINCE
You are everything maidens could wish for!

CINDERELLA'S PRINCE
Then why no—?

RAPUNZEL'S PRINCE
Do I know?

CINDERELLA'S PRINCE

The girl must be mad.

RAPUNZEL'S PRINCE

You know nothing of madness
Till you're climbing her hair
And you see her up there
As you're nearing her,
All the while hearing her
"Ah-ah-ah-ah-ah-ah-ah-ah—"

BOTH

Agony!

CINDERELLA'S PRINCE

Misery!

RAPUNZEL'S PRINCE

Woe!

BOTH

Though it's different for each.

CINDERELLA'S PRINCE

Always ten steps behind—

RAPUNZEL'S PRINCE

Always ten feet below—

BOTH
And she's just out of reach.
Agony
That can cut like a knife!

I must have her to wife.

Moments in the Woods

Was that me?
Was that him?
Did a prince really kiss me?
And kiss me?
And kiss me?
And did I kiss him back?

Was it wrong?
Am I mad?
Is that all?
Does he miss me?
Was he suddenly
Getting bored with me?

Wake up! Stop dreaming.
Stop prancing about the woods.
It's not beseeming.
What is it about the woods?

Back to life, back to sense,
Back to child, back to husband,
No one lives in the woods.
There are vows, there are ties,
There are needs, there are standards,
There are shouldn'ts and shoulds.

Why not both instead?
There's the answer, if you're clever:
Have a child for warmth
And a baker for bread,
And a prince for whatever—
Never!
It's these woods.

Face the facts, find the boy,
Join the group, stop the Giant,
Just get out of these woods.
Was that him? Yes, it was.
Was that me? No, it wasn't,
Just a trick of the woods.

Just a moment,
One peculiar passing moment . . .

Must it all be either less or more,
Either plain or grand?
Is it always "or"?
Is it never "and"?
That's what woods are for:
For those moments in the woods.

Oh, if life were made of moments,
Even now and then a bad one—!
But if life were only moments,
Then you'd never know you had one.

First a witch, then a child,
Then a prince, then a moment—
Who can live in the woods?
And to get what you wish,
Only just for a moment—
These are dangerous woods . . .

Let the moment go.
Don't forget it for a moment, though.
Just remembering you've had an "and"
When you're back to "or"
Makes the "or" mean more
Than it did before.
Now I understand—
And it's time to leave the woods!

On the Steps of the Palace

CINDERELLA

He's a very smart prince.
He's a prince who prepares.
Knowing this time I'd run from him,
He spread pitch on the stairs.
I was caught unawares.
And I thought: Well, he cares—
This is more than just malice.
Better stop and take stock
While you're standing here stuck
On the steps of the palace.

You think, what do you want?
You think, make a decision.
Why not stay and be caught?
You think, well, it's a thought,
What would be his response?
But then what if he knew
Who you were when you know
That you're not what he thinks
That he wants?

And then what if you are
What a prince would envision?
Although how can you know
Who you are till you know
What you want, which you don't?

So then which do you pick:
Where you're safe, out of sight,
And yourself, but where everything's wrong?
Or where everything's right
And you know that you'll never belong?

And whichever you pick,
Do it quick,
'Cause you're starting to stick
To the steps of the palace.

It's your first big decision,
The choice isn't easy to make.
To arrive at a ball
Is exciting and all—
Once you're there, though, it's scary.

And it's fun to deceive
When you know you can leave,
But you have to be wary.

There's a lot that's at stake,
But you've stalled long enough,
'Cause you're still standing stuck
In the stuff on the steps . . .

Better run along home
And avoid the collision.
Even though they don't care,
You'll be better off there

Where there's nothing to choose,
So there's nothing to lose.
So you pry up your shoes.

Then from out of the blue,
And without any guide,
You know what your decision is,
Which is not to decide.
You'll just leave him a clue:
For example, a shoe.
And then see what he'll do.

Now it's he and not you
Who is stuck with a shoe,
In a stew,
In the goo,
And you've learned something, too,
Something you never knew,
On the steps of the palace!

Children Will Listen

Sometimes people leave you
Halfway through the wood.
Do not let it grieve you,
No one leaves for good.
You are not alone.
No one is alone.

Hold him to the light now,
Let him see the glow.
Things will be all right now.
Tell him what you know . . .

WITCH

Careful the things you say,
Children will listen.
Careful the things you do,
Children will see.
And learn.

Guide them along the way,
Children will glisten.
Children will look to you
For which way to turn,
To learn what to be.

Careful before you say,
"Listen to me."
Children will listen.

ALL

Careful the wish you make,
Wishes are children.
Careful the path they take—
Wishes come true,
Not free.

Careful the spell you cast,
Not just on children.
Sometimes the spell may last
Past what you can see
And turn against you . . .

WITCH

Careful the tale you tell.
That is the spell.
Children will listen . . .

ALL

Though it's fearful,
Though it's deep, though it's dark
And though you may lose the path,
Though you may encounter wolves,
You can't just act,
You have to listen.
You can't just act,
You have to think.

There are always wolves,
There are always spells,

There are always beans,
Or a giant dwells
There,
So:
Into the woods you go again,
You have to every now and then.
Into the woods, no telling when,
Be ready for the journey.

Into the woods, but not too fast,
Or what you wish you lose at last.
Into the woods, but mind the past.
Into the woods, but mind the future.
Into the woods, but not to stray
Or tempt the Wolf
Or steal from the Giant.

The way is dark,
The light is dim,
But now there's you,
Me, her and him.
The chances look small,
The choices look grim,
But everything you learn there
Will help when you return there.

BAKER, CINDERELLA, JACK,
LITTLE RED RIDING HOOD
(*Softly*)
The light is getting dimmer—

BAKER
I think I see a glimmer—

ALL
Into the woods—you have to grope,
But that's the way you learn to cope.
Into the woods to find there's hope
Of getting through the journey.

Into the woods, each time you go,
There's more to learn of what you know.
Into the woods, but not too slow—
Into the woods, it's nearing midnight—
Into the woods to mind the Wolf,
To heed the Witch,
To honor the Giant,
To mind,
To heed,
To find,
To think,
To teach,
To join,
To go to the Festival!

Into the woods,
Into the woods,
Into the woods,
Then out of the woods—
And happy ever after!

CINDERELLA
I wish . . .

ASSASSINS

The Ballad of Booth

BALLADEER

Someone tell the story,
Someone sing the song.
Every now and then the country
Goes a little wrong.
Every now and then a madman's
Bound to come along.
Doesn't stop the story—
Story's pretty strong.
Doesn't change the song . . .

Johnny Booth was a handsome devil,
Got up in his rings and fancy silks.
Had him a temper, but kept it level.
Everybody called him Wilkes.

Why did you do it, Johnny?
Nobody agrees.
You who had everything,
What made you bring
A nation to its knees?

Some say it was your voice had gone,
Some say it was booze.
They say you killed a country, John,
Because of bad reviews.

Johnny lived, with a grace and glitter,
Kinda like the lives he lived onstage.
Died in a barn, in pain and bitter,
Twenty-seven years of age.

Why did you do it, Johnny,
Throw it all away?
Why did you do it, boy,
Not just destroy
The pride and joy
Of Illinois,
But all the U.S.A.?

Your brother made you jealous, John,
You couldn't fill his shoes.
Was that the reason, tell us, John—
Along with bad reviews?

They say your ship was sinkin', John . . .
You'd started missing cues . . .
They say it wasn't Lincoln, John.
You'd merely had
A slew of bad
Reviews—

He said,
"Damn you, Lincoln,
You had your way—

BOOTH

Tell them, boy!

BALLADEER

—With blood you drew
Out of blue and gray!"

BOOTH

Tell it all!
Tell them till they listen!

BALLADEER

He said,
"Damn you, Lincoln,
And damn the day
You threw the "U" out
Of U.S.A.!"
He said:

BOOTH

Hunt me down, smear my name,
Say I did it for the fame,
What I did was kill the man who killed
   my country.
Now the southland will mend.
Now this bloody war can end,
Because someone slew the tyrant,
Just as Brutus slew the tyrant—

BALLADEER
He said:

BALLADEER, BOOTH
Damn you, Lincoln,
You righteous whore!

BOOTH
Tell 'em!
Tell 'em what he did!

BALLADEER, BOOTH
You turned your spite
Into civil war!

BOOTH
Tell 'em!
Tell 'em the truth!

BALLADEER
And more . . .

BOOTH
Tell 'em, boy!
Tell 'em how it happened,
How the end doesn't mean that it's over,
How surrender is not the end!
Tell them:

How the country is not what it was,
Where there's blood on the clover,

How the nation can never again
Be the hope that it was,
How the bruises may never be healed,
How the wounds are forever,
How we gave up the field
But we still wouldn't yield,
How the union can never recover
From that vulgar,
High and mighty
Nigger lover,
Never—!
Never. Never. Never.
No, the country is not what it was . . .

The sound of crackling flames. Smoke begins to seep under the walls of the barn. Booth bows his head in prayer.

BOOTH

Damn my soul if you must,
Let my body turn to dust,
Let it mingle with the ashes of the country.
Let them curse me to hell,
Leave it to history to tell:
What I did, I did well,
And I did it for my country.

Let them cry, "Dirty traitor!"
They will understand it later.
The country is not what it was . . .

BALLADEER
Johnny Booth was a headstrong fellow,
Even he believed the things he said.
Some called him noble, some said yellow.
What he was was off his head.

How could you do it, Johnny,
Calling it a cause?
You left a legacy
Of butchery
And treason we
Took eagerly,
And thought you'd get applause.

But traitors just get jeers and boos,
Not visits to their graves,
While Lincoln, who got mixed reviews,
Because of you, John, now gets only raves.

Damn you, Johnny!
You paved the way
For other madmen
To make us pay.
Lots of madmen
Have had their say—
But only for a day.

Listen to the stories.
Hear it in the songs.
Angry men don't write the rules,
And guns don't right the wrongs.
Hurts a while, but soon the country's
Back where it belongs,
And that's the truth.

Still and all,
Damn you, Booth!

The Ballard of Czolgosz

BALLADEER

Czolgosz,
Working man,
Born in the middle of Michigan,
Woke with a thought and away he ran
To the Pan-American Exposition
In Buffalo,
In Buffalo.

Saw of a sudden how things were run,
Said, "Time's a-wasting, it's Nineteen-One.
Some men have everything and some have none,
So rise and shine.
In the U.S.A.
You can work your way
To the head of the line!"

Czolgosz,
Quiet man,
Worked out a quiet and simple plan,
Strolled of a morning, all spick and span,
To the Temple of Music
By the Tower of Light
At the Pan-American Exposition
In Buffalo,
In Buffalo.

Saw Bill McKinley there in the sun.

Heard Bill McKinley say, "Folks, have fun!
Some men have everything and some have none,
But that's just fine:
In the U.S.A.
You can work your way
To the head of the line!"

FAIRGOERS
Big Bill—!

BALLADEER
—Gave 'em a thrill.

FAIRGOERS
Big Bill—!

BALLADEER
—Sold 'em a bill.

FAIRGOERS
Big Bill—!

BALLADEER
Who'd want to kill
A man of good will
Like—?

FAIRGOERS, BALLADEER
Big Bill!

BALLADEER
Czolgosz,

Angry man,
Said, "I will do what a poor man can.
Yes, and there's nowhere more fitting than
In the Temple of Music
By the Tower of Light
Between the Fountain of Abundance
And the Court of Lilies
At the great Pan-American Exposition
In Buffalo,
In Buffalo."

Wrapped him a handkerchief 'round his gun,
Said, "Nothin' wrong about what I done.
Some men have everything and some have
    none—
That's by design.
The idea wasn't mine alone, but mine—
And that's the sign:

In the U.S.A.
You can have your say,
You can set your goals
And seize the day,
You've been given the freedom
To work your way
To the head of the line—

To the head of the line!"

The Ballad of Guiteau

GUITEAU

I am going to the Lordy.
I am so glad.
I am going to the Lordy,
I am so glad.
I am going to the Lordy,
Glory hallelujah!
Glory hallelujah!
I am going to the Lordy . . .

BALLADEER

Come all ye Christians,
And learn from a sinner:
Charlie Guiteau.
Bound and determined
He'd wind up a winner,
Charlie had dreams
That he wouldn't let go.
Said, "Nothing to it,
I want it, I'll do it,
I'm Charles J. Guiteau."

Charlie Guiteau
Never said "never"
Or heard the word "no."
Faced with disaster,
His heart would beat faster,

His smile would just grow,
And he'd say:

Look on the bright side,
Look on the bright side,
Sit on the right side
Of the Lord!
This is the land of
Opportunity.
He is your lightning,
You His sword.

Wait till you see tomorrow,
Tomorrow you'll get your reward!
You can be sad
Or you can be President.
Look on the bright side . . .

I am going to the Lordy . . .

BALLADEER
Charlie Guiteau
Drew a crowd to his trial,
Led them in prayer,
Said, "I killed Garfield,
I'll make no denial.
I was just acting
For Someone up there.
The Lord's my employer,

200

And now He's my lawyer,
So do what you dare."

Charlie said, "Hell,
If I am guilty,
Then God is as well."
But God was acquitted
And Charlie committed
Until he should hang.
Still, he sang:

GUITEAU

Look on the bright side,
Not on the black side.
Get off your backside,
Shine those shoes!
This is your golden
Opportunity:
You are the lightning
And you're news!

Wait till you see tomorrow,
Tomorrow you won't be ignored!
You could be pardoned,
You could be President.
Look on the bright side . . .

I am going to the Lordy . . .

BALLADEER
Charlie Guiteau
Had a crowd at the scaffold—

GUITEAU
I am so glad . . .

BALLADEER
—Filled up the square,
So many people
That tickets were raffled.
Shine on his shoes,
Charlie mounted the stair,
Said, "Never sorrow,
Just wait till tomorrow,
Today isn't fair.
Don't despair . . ."

GUITEAU
Look on the bright side,
Look on the bright side,
Sit on the right side—
—Of the—
I am going to the Lordy,
I am so glad!
I am going to the Lordy,
I am so glad!
I have unified my party,
I have saved my country.

I shall be remembered!
I am going to the Lordy . . .

BALLADEER
Look on the bright side,
Not on the sad side,
Inside the bad side
Something's good!
This is your golden
Opportunity:
You've been a preacher—

GUITEAU
Yes, I have!

BALLADEER
You've been an author—

GUITEAU
Yes, I have!

BALLADEER
You've been a killer—

GUITEAU
Yes, I have!

BALLADEER
You could be an angel—

GUITEAU
Yes, I could!

BALLADEER

Just wait until tomorrow,
Tomorrow they'll all climb aboard!
What if you never
Got to be President?
You'll be remembered—

Look on the bright side—

(*Again*)

Trust in tomorrow—

(*Once more*)

GUITEAU, BALLADEER

And the Lord!

DICK TRACY

What Can You Lose?

88 KEYS
What can you lose?
Only the blues.
Why keep concealing
Everything you're feeling?
Say it to her—
What can you lose?
Maybe it shows—
She's had clues,
Which she chose to ignore.
Maybe, though, she knows,
And just wants to go on as before—
As a friend, nothing more.
So she closes the door.

BREATHLESS
Well, if she does,
Those are the dues.

BOTH
Once the words are spoken,
Something may be broken—
Still, you love her,
What can you lose?

88 KEYS
But what if she goes?
At least, now you have part of her—

BOTH
What if she had to choose?

BREATHLESS
Leave it alone.

88 KEYS
Hold it all in.

BOTH
Better a bone.
Don't even begin.
With so much to win,
There's too much to lose.

More

BREATHLESS
Once upon a time I had plenty of nothing—
Which was fine with me,
Because I had rhythm, music, love,
The sun, the stars, and the moon above,
Had the clear blue sky and the deep blue sea.
That was when the best things in life were free.

Then time went by and now I got plenty
    of plenty—
Which is fine with me,
'Cause I still got love, I still got rhythm,
But look at what I got to go with 'em!

"Who could ask for anything more?"
I hear you query.
Who could ask for anything more?
Well, let me tell you,
Dearie:

Got my diamonds, got my yacht,
Got a guy I adore.
I'm so happy with what I've got,
I want more!

Count your blessings: one, two, three—
I just hate keeping score.

Any number is fine with me,
As long as it's more!

As long as it's more . . .

I'm no mathematician.
All I know is addition.
I find counting a bore.
Keep the number mounting,
Your accountant does the counting . . .

CHORUS GIRLS
More! More!

BREATHLESS
I got rhythm, music too,
Just as much as before.
Got my guy and my sky of blue,
Now, however, I own the view.
More is better than nothing, true,
But nothing's better than
More, more, more,
Nothing's better than more!

One is fun,
Why not two?
And if you like two,
Might as well have four.
And if you like four,

Why not a few,
Why not a slew

More?
More!

If you've got a little,
Why not a lot?
Add a bit and it'll
Get to be an oodle.
Every jot and tittle
Adds to the pot—
Soon you've got the kit
As well as the caboodle—

More! More! More! More!

Never say when,
Never stop at plenty—
If it's gonna rain, let it pour.
Happy with ten,
Happier with twenty—
If you like a penny,
Wouldn't you like many
Much more?

Or does that sound too greedy?
That's not greed – no, indeed,
That's just stocking the store.
Gotta fill your cupboard—
Remember Mother Hubbard!

CHORUS GIRLS
More! More!

BREATHLESS
Each possession you possess
Helps your spirits to soar,
That's what's soothing about excess—
Never settle for something less.
Something's better than nothing, yes—

CHORUS GIRLS
But nothing's better than
More, more, more—

BREATHLESS
Except all, all, all . . .

CHORUS GIRLS
Except all, all, all . . .

BREATHLESS
Except once you have it all—

CHORUS GIRLS
Have it all—

BREATHLESS
You may find, all else above—

CHORUS GIRLS
Else above—

BREATHLESS
That though "things" are bliss,
There's one thing you miss,
And that's—

ALL
More! More!
More more more more more!!

PASSION

I Wish I Could Forget You

FOSCA

I wish I could forget you,
Erase you from my mind.
But ever since I met you,
I find
I cannot leave the thought of you behind.

I know that I've upset you.
I know I've been unkind.
I wanted you to vanish from sight,
But now I see you in a different light.
And though I cannot love you,
I wish that I could love you.

For now I'm seeing love
Like none I've ever known,
A love as pure as breath,
As permanent as death,
Implacable as stone.

A love that like a knife
Has cut into a life
I wanted left alone.
A love I may regret,
But one I can't forget.

I don't know how I let you
So far inside my mind,
But there you are and there you will stay.
How could I ever wish you away?
I see now I was blind.
And should you die tomorrow,
Another thing I see:
Your love will live in me.

BOUNCE

The Game
(*Reprise*)

WILSON

Easy come and easy go,
Why get so upset?
Every high spot has a low—
Can't afford regret.

Win one minute, lose the next,
Everything's a sequel.
Think of them as equal:
Place another bet.
Find another table and forget.

The only thing that matters is the game.
The trick is getting back into the game.
You win, you lose, it's over with.
Don't stick with it, it's gone.
Close shop.
Move on.

Life's full of disappointment,
As you know.
You have to keep inventing
As you go.

Papa said,
"Don't be blind.
Look ahead,
Not behind.
Find a new frontier
And stake another claim."
The only thing that matters is the game.

"Addie Mizner, Architect"—
It's as good as signed.
Failure seen in retrospect
Is just a state of mind.

Look at me, I lose a wife,
Then a protégé, right?
Next day I'm a playwright!
When you're in a bind,
Close the book
And just don't look
Behind.

The Game
(*Version 2*)

WILSON

Never let a chance go by, Addie,
Isn't that what Papa said?
When you see it, grab it,
Soon it's like a habit.
Now and then you miss one,
But I guarantee you this one
Is a winner.
I'm no longer a beginner . . .

Addie, take the chance
Or it disappears!
Every card you're dealt opens new frontiers—
Let's be pioneers!

ADDISON

We could lose everything we've worked for!

WILSON

Exactly!

It's more than just the money, it's the game.
The thing that really matters is the game.
That moment when the card is turned
And nothing is the same—
Then bang!
New game!

The fact remains, when all is said and done,
The fun is in the winning, not what's won.
What you've made, what you've spent,
That is not the main event.
With every hand you stake a whole new claim.
The only thing that matters is the game.

Better than girls, better than booze,
Beating ace high with a pair of twos.
Better to win, but if you lose,
You've had that moment!

Better than smoke, better than snuff,
Hooking a sucker just enough,
Betting your bundle on a bluff,
Jesus, what a moment!
Still, the point, as I keep saying, is the game.
Not just the hand you're playing, but the game.
And what's around the corner,
If by chance you lose your pants?
New deal,
New chance!

It's never really money that's at stake.
That's nice, but it's just icing on the cake.
It's your life, every pot,
What you are, not what you've got.
Compared to that, the world seems pretty tame.
The only thing that matters is the game.